EXECUTIVE SUMMARY

Most colleges and universities aspire to produce graduates who think critically, who can make judgments in complex situations on the basis of sound reason, adequate evidence, and articulated values. Why, then, does criticism such as that of Allan Bloom in *The Closing of the American Mind* strike such a responsive chord with the American public? Is it true, as the subtitle of Bloom's book proclaims, that "higher education has failed democracy and impoverished the souls of today's students"?

Bloom's sweeping claim does not lend itself well to empirical validation or disconfirmation (Bloom himself disdains empiricism as a path to truth). Nonetheless, theoretical and empirical studies of students' intellectual development are helpful in addressing several questions: What is critical thinking? How does it develop? What role does knowledge play in critical thinking? Do educational practices affect the ability to think critically? This report surveys theory, research, teaching practice, and institutional programs pertinent to these questions.

Does Higher Education Promote Critical Thinking?
Three perspectives dominate current literature on critical thinking and its development in college: argument skills, cognitive processes, and intellectual development.

Argument skills
Introductory courses on critical thinking teach students to detect and avoid fallacious reasoning and to analyze deductive and inductive arguments. These courses are grounded in informal logic, a branch of philosophy. Argument skills improve modestly with college experience (McMillan 1987), but education has only a minor effect on the depth of students' arguments on everyday issues (Perkins 1986). It may be because subject matter knowledge is more important in critical thinking than generic knowledge of how to analyze arguments (McPeck 1981). Or it may be because students are unable to make use of knowledge that is in fact available to them (Perkins 1986).

Cognitive processes
Cognitive psychologists study the organization of knowledg memory and its role in tasks such as reading, writing, and problem solving. In cognitive terms, critical thinking is pro lem solving in situations where "solutions" cannot be verifi empirically. Confronted with a complex issue, the learner con-

structs a representation or mental model of the situation; the model is organized around a claim or thesis and supported by reasoning and evidence.

Three kinds of knowledge interact in developing a model: (1) *declarative knowledge*, knowing the facts and concepts in the discipline; (2) *procedural knowledge*, knowing how to reason, inquire, and present knowledge in the discipline; and (3) *metacognition*, cognitive control strategies, such as setting goals, determining when additional information is needed, and assessing the fruitfulness of a line of inquiry.

Experts draw on an extensive network of hierarchically and causally organized declarative knowledge relevant to problems in their field. In addition, they use metacognition and the reasoning procedures of their discipline; however, their use of these cognitive processes is so automatic that they may be unaware of the skill that underlies their performance.

Students acquire considerable declarative knowledge in their college courses. Their knowledge, however, may not be effectively organized for solving particular problems. Moreover, procedural knowledge is rarely taught (in part because it is tacit knowledge for professors), and many students' metacognitive skills are poorly developed. As a result, students may not draw upon the full extent of their knowledge when called upon to complete assignments that require critical thinking.

This report summarizes cognitive research on thinking in various disciplines and describes courses that foster critical thinking in the disciplines. Many of these courses explicitly teach discipline-specific procedural knowledge and build metacognitive processes into instructions for assignments and class activities.

Intellectual development

While cognitive researchers focus on learners' discipline- or even task-specific knowledge of complex issues, the developmental approach traces transformations in students' beliefs about the nature of knowledge and truth. A major developmental task for college students is discovering and reckoning with the loss of singular truth and ultimate authority (Belenky et al. 1986; Perry 1970).

Many people assume that knowledge consists of objective facts possessed by authorities. When students encounter pluralism, complexity, and uncertainty in college courses, they interpret it as "subjectivity." They proclaim that when "facts" are

Critical Thinking:
Theory, Research, Practice, and Possibilities

by Joanne Gainen Kurfiss

ASHE-ERIC Higher Education Report No. 2, 1988

Prepared by

 *Clearinghouse on Higher Education*
The George Washington University

Published by

 *Association for the Study of*
Higher Education

Jonathan D. Fife,
Series Editor

Cite as
Kurfiss, Joanne G. *Critical Thinking: Theory, Research, Practice, and Possibilities.* ASHE-ERIC Higher Education Report No. 2. Washington, D.C.: Association for the Study of Higher Education, 1988.

Library of Congress Catalog Card Number 88-71519
ISSN 0884-0040
ISBN 0-913317-44–6

Managing Editor: Christopher Rigaux
Manuscript Editor: Barbara Fishel/Editech
Cover design by Michael David Brown, Rockville, Maryland

The ERIC Clearinghouse on Higher Education invites individuals to submit proposals for writing monographs for the Higher Education Report series. Proposals must include:
1. A detailed manuscript proposal of not more than five pages.
2. A chapter-by-chapter outline.
3. A 75-word summary to be used by several review committees for the initial screening and rating of each proposal.
4. A vita.
5. A writing sample.

ERIC **Clearinghouse on Higher Education**
School of Education and Human Development
The George Washington University
One Dupont Circle, Suite 630
Washington, D.C. 20036-1183

ASHE **Association for the Study of Higher Education**
Texas A&M University
Department of Educational Administration
Harrington Education Center
College Station, Texas 77843

This publication was prepared partially with funding from the Office of Educational Research and Improvement, U.S. Department of Education, under contract no. ED RI-88-062014. The opinions expressed in this report do not necessarily reflect the positions or policies of OERI or the Department.

not known, all opinions are equally valid. This view (called "multiplicity" or "subjective knowledge") is similar to the excessive "openness" deplored by Allan Bloom. Several developmental studies support Bloom's contention that students view knowledge as "purely" subjective.

Persistent attention to the justification of belief helps students progress to the view that opinions are knowledge claims that have stronger or weaker grounds and that their merits can be discussed (though perhaps not agreed upon) within a particular intellectual community. The final developmental task is to make rational, caring commitments in a relativistic world. For many educators, it is the mature epistemology of commitment, not isolated analytical skills, that is the true aim of instruction for critical thinking.

Developmentally effective instruction *challenges* students to confront the indeterminacy of knowledge at the level just beyond their present understanding and *supports* them by affirming what they have already achieved (Belenky et al. 1986; Widick, Knefelkamp, and Parker 1975). The intellectual development perspective has been extensively investigated and has provided guidance and inspiration for many educators.

What Can Educators Do to Foster Critical Thinking?
This report describes numerous examples of programs and courses that successfully integrate critical thinking with content learning in many disciplines. Many of these projects overcome students' reluctance to tackle challenging assignments by connecting themes, values, and modes of inquiry in the discipline with experiences and questions that are meaningful in students' lives (Gamson and Associates 1984; Loacker et al. 1984). These courses do not neglect "content" in favor of "process." Rather, they require students to *use* content in projects that require critical thinking. Students' initial attempts are recognized as the work of novices, to be developed and refined as their base of declarative and strategic knowledge grows. Teachers in such courses often use structured small group work in which students clarify concepts, explore complex problems, debate issues, and get help on work in progress.

Fostering all students' critical thinking abilities and intellectual development requires the participation and support of faculty in every discipline. Institutional approaches currently in use include freshman-year programs, cross-curricular models, and assessment-based strategies. To build support for institutional cooperation, campus leaders often survey faculty, employers, or alumni or conduct a formal assessment of thinking skills, then create a forum for discussion and interpretation of the results. Once courses or programs are established, administrators must recognize that faculty who are experimenting with new teaching methods and skills need support in the form of resources, time, training, and encouragement. Supportive administrators often find that teaching for thinking is an important source of faculty vitality, renewal, and collegiality (Gamson and Associates 1984).

Recommendations for the Future

Support for research, practice, and dissemination of critical thinking pedagogy is needed from a variety of sources to strengthen critical thinking in higher education. Collaborations between cognitive researchers and faculty will deepen understanding of learning and thinking in every discipline. Academic and professional organizations can play an important role by sponsoring research and instructional projects on critical thinking and related topics, such as ethical reasoning.

Critical thinking is an essential capacity of citizens in a healthy democratic society, and postsecondary educators are uniquely qualified to cultivate this capacity among students. Attention to critical thinking is not an educational panacea, and many other capacities of young adults and other students also deserve the attention of educators. To the degree, however, that critical thinking contributes to a more rational and humane society, its cultivation merits a significant expenditure of educators' collective time, wisdom, and effort. The research and practice summarized in this report provide a point of departure as well as a reason to hope that the work will prove rewarding for those who accept the challenge.

ADVISORY BOARD

CONSULTING EDITORS

Charles Adams
Director, The Inquiry Program
Center for the Study of Adult and Higher Education
University of Massachusetts

Ann E. Austin
Research Assistant Professor
Vanderbilt University

Trudy W. Banta
Research Professor
University of Tennessee

Harriet W. Cabell
Associate Dean for Adult Education
Director, External Degree Program
University of Alabama

L. Leon Campbell
Provost and Vice President for Academic Affairs
University of Delaware

Ellen Earle Chaffee
Associate Commissioner for Academic Affairs
North Dakota State Board of Higher Education

Robert Paul Churchill
Chair and Associate Professor
Department of Philosophy
George Washington University

Peter T. Ewell
Senior Associate
National Center for Higher Education Management Systems

Reynolds Ferrante
Professor of Higher Education
George Washington University

Zelda F. Gamson
Director
New England Resource Center for Higher Education

J. Wade Gilley
Senior Vice President
George Mason University

David A. Kolb
Professor and Chairman
Department of Organizational Behavior
The Weatherhead School of Management
Case Western Reserve University

Oscar T. Lenning
Vice President for Academic Affairs
Robert Wesleyan College

Charles J. McClain
President
Northeast Missouri State University

Judith B. McLaughlin
Research Associate on Education and Sociology
Harvard University

Marcia Mentkowski
Director of Research and Evaluation
Professor of Psychology
Alverno College

James L. Morrison
Professor
University of North Carolina

Sheila A. Murdick
Director, National Program on Noncollegiate-Sponsored
 Instruction
New York State Board of Regents

Elizabeth M. Nuss
Executive Director
National Association of Student Personnel Administrators

Robert L. Payton
Director, Center on Philanthropy
Indiana University

Jack E. Rossmann
Professor of Psychology
Macalester College

Donald M. Sacken
Associate Professor
University of Arizona

Robert A. Scott
President
Ramapo College of New Jersey

Henry A. Spille
Director, Office on Educational Credits and Credentials
American Council on Education

CONTENTS

FOREWORD

A person's thinking style is developed over a long period of time. It is generally the result of three factors: (1) a natural inclination toward a particular thinking style, such as right-brain or left-brain; (2) modelling, through such mechanisms as trial-and-error and positive reinforcement; and (3) the formal education process. The concern of this report is with the third factor, i.e., the formal development of critical thinking.

The first question concerning critical thinking is not can or how it can be taught, but whether it is allowed to be taught? The popular press is filled with reports on how parents and organizations try to prevent the teaching of ideas that are contrary to their own beliefs. An example of this appeared in the *Washington Post* on October 20, 1988, in an article about how a curriculum program, "Facing History and Ourselves," used the history of the Holocaust to explore morality, human behavior, law, and citizenship; it was opposed by a concerned organization who objected to students being encouraged to think critically about decisions made by their government.

A second question is whether teachers have the internal support to teach critical thinking. Critical thinking is often opposed by students themselves because of its difficulty. As Henry Ford is quoted as saying, "Thinking is hard work, and that's why so few people do it." Critical thinking is very hard to quantify or grade, and the grading of critical thinking is always subject to debate. It is easier and safer for faculty to teach at a level that is less threatening and more quantifiable.

The importance critical thinking plays in the education process depends upon one's philosophic belief in the purpose of education. If education is only to teach basic facts, than critical thinking plays only a minor role and rote learning is sufficient. If, however, the role of education is to develop greater reasoning skill in order to cope with and make decisions about life and society, then critical thinking plays a central position, since reasoning is impossible without critical thinking.

Because critical thinking is generally not encouraged at the elementary and secondary level, it becomes a central responsibility for higher education. In this report, Joanne Gainen Kurfiss, a teaching consultant at the University of Delaware, examines critical thinking on the three levels by which it is most commonly taught in higher education: argument skills, cognitive processes, intellectual development. One of the most difficult features of teaching critical thinking is incorporating it

---

into the basic curiculum; the author provides a wealth of excellent suggestions on how this can be accomplished.

One thing that almost everyone will agree on is that the next 50 years will bring more changes than has been seen in the sum history of humanity. How well society handles them in a large part will be determined by its ability to reason and think critically. This report clearly provides guidance in helping faculty insure that critical thinking becomes an integral part of learning.

Jonathan D. Fife
Professor and Director
ERIC Clearinghouse on Higher Education
School of Education and Human Development
The George Washington University

ACKNOWLEDGMENTS

This project has benefited from my work in the Center for Teaching Effectiveness and especially from conversations with my colleague in the center, Julie Schmidt.

The project also benefited from data base searches provided by ERIC and from generous sharing of reprints by many researchers and teachers. Mary Norton, who teaches critical thinking, graciously provided resources for the chapter on argument skills. My thanks to all, including those whose work ultimately fell outside the scope of this report.

I also want to thank my first readers, who include Jon Fife and Chris Rigaux at the ERIC Clearinghouse, the reviewers of the original manuscript, and participants at the University of Chicago's Institute on Teaching and Learning in May 1988, who read an early version of the materials on theoretical perspectives. Their questions challenged my thinking, and their interest supported my faith that the effort was worthwhile.

This book is dedicated to my family.

INTRODUCTION

In recent years, critical thinking has become a major focus of conferences, publications, and programs in higher education. Schools and colleges from New York to California have established programs and centers devoted to critical thinking. Dozens of conference papers have been presented in forums across the country, and new books on the subject are appearing at an accelerating rate. Critical thinking skills are tested statewide in California public schools (Kneedler 1985). And many institutions have received grants to support projects on critical thinking.

Why all this attention to critical thinking?

The complexities of contemporary life place great demands on human rationality; about this there is little disagreement. Contemporary problems are not simply larger or more numerous than those of the past, however; they must be resolved in a world where familiar assumptions (like continued growth and expansion) no longer hold true (Morrill 1980). Furthermore, it is human *irrationality*, not a lack of knowledge, that threatens human potential (Nickerson 1986c).

It is human irrationality, not a lack of knowledge, that threatens human potential.

Against this background is the increasingly compelling evidence of serious deficiencies in the ability to reason among college students and the limited influence of college education on critical thinking skills. Depth of argument on controversial topics is minimal and increases marginally as a result of college instruction (Perkins 1985). Seniors are more adept than freshmen at evaluating position papers, but their overall level of performance is low (Keeley, Browne, and Kreutzer 1982). Compared to freshmen, seniors in liberal arts and engineering are more aware of evidence in reasoning, but they still believe judgment is a matter of "individual idiosyncracies" (Welfel 1982, p. 495). College students make judgments on the basis of unexamined personal preferences, even after four years of higher education (Belenky et al. 1986; King et al. 1983; Welfel 1982).

Longitudinal studies show an influence of education, but when reasoning about everyday questions, such as bias in the news and evaluation of food additives, only graduate students seem to recognize that different points of view can be compared and evaluated through contextual reasoning (King et al. 1983; King, Kitchener, and Wood 1985). Many researchers have documented an uncritical, "makes-sense epistemology" (Perkins, Allen, and Hafner 1983), termed "multiplicity" (Perry 1970) and "subjective knowledge" (Belenky et al.

1986). Recently, college students' subjectivism has become the focus of national attention as "the openness of indifference" described in *The Closing of the American Mind* (Bloom 1987, p. 41).

Disheartening reports and personal observation of students have prompted educators and researchers to take a closer look at students' reasoning and to search for teaching methods to encourage critical thinking. Their successes, frustrations, and unresolved questions are the subject of this report.

Definition of Terms

Critical thinking is a rational response to questions that cannot be answered definitively and for which all the relevant information may not be available. It is defined here as *an investigation whose purpose is to explore a situation, phenomenon, question, or problem to arrive at a hypothesis or conclusion about it that integrates all available information and that can therefore be convincingly justified.* In critical thinking, all assumptions are open to question, divergent views are aggressively sought, and the inquiry is not biased in favor of a particular outcome.

The outcomes of a critical inquiry are twofold: a *conclusion* (or hypothesis) and the *justification* offered in support of it. These outcomes are usually set forth in the form of an *argument*, defined as "the sequence of interlinked claims and reasons that, between them, establish the content and force of the position for which a particular speaker is arguing" (Toulmin, Rieke, and Janik 1979, p. 13). The need for justification arises from the ill-defined nature of problems to which the term "critical thinking" generally applies. Because conclusions cannot be tested (as they can be in problem solving), the arguer must demonstrate their plausibility by offering supporting reasons (Voss, Tyler, and Yengo 1983).

The inquiry itself, in which evidence is reviewed and interpreted, is sometimes referred to as "the context of *discovery*"; it is the inventive, creative phase of critical thinking. The presentation of the argument is referred to as "the context of *justification*" (Kahane 1980; McPeck 1981). In practice, the two may be intertwined rather than distinct.

Academic and professional settings offer numerous occasions for critical thinking. A student offering evidence from a literary text to support an insight about the author's intentions is engaged in critical thinking (the context of justification). Students investigating divergent accounts of a historical event and attempting to formulate a plausible interpretation of what really happened or to decipher the meaning of events are engaged in critical thinking (the context of discovery). Faculty studying a new curriculum proposal are engaged in critical thinking. In each case, the quality of the inquiry depends on the degree to which the inquirers are able to set aside preconceptions and remain open to new information or plausible counterarguments.

Critical thinking can result in a decision, a speech, a proposal or experiment, or a document like a position paper. It can result in a new way of approaching significant issues in one's life or a deeper understanding of the basis for one's actions (Brookfield 1987). Or it might also result in political activity (Guyton 1982, 1984).

While critical thinking may yield a satisfying account of the issue or subject in question, it might also raise doubts that cannot be resolved under the particular circumstances of the inquiry, especially when moral or ethical principles are at stake. When an account is constructed, the individual must often act upon it even while recognizing that it is subject to further development and may change in light of new evidence or reasoning or a change in circumstances (Perry 1970).

The Challenge of Teaching Critical Thinking
Educators in every discipline value critical thinking skills of one form or another. Asked to identify the reasoning skills most critical to success in graduate school in their disciplines, professors in six disciplines offered only partially overlapping lists (Powers and Enright 1987). For example, chemists most value the ability to draw sound inferences from observations, critically analyze and evaluate previous research, and generate new questions or experiments, while English professors most value the ability to elaborate an argument and develop its implications, understand, analyze, and evaluate arguments, support general assertions with details, and recognize the central thesis in a work. For English professors, the most critical errors include inability to synthesize ideas, unquestioning acceptance of assumptions, and reliance on narration or description when analysis is appropriate. In education, a serious error is failing to evaluate the credibility or reliability of a source (Powers and Enright 1987, p. 669).

Although these skills are valued, they are seldom explicitly taught to students. Professors display the *products* of their skills in the form of the arguments and interpretations they present in lectures and discussions. But students rarely witness the *processes* by which their professors interrogate texts, compare conflicting interpretations of phenomena or works of art or literature, or discover patterns in seemingly chaotic evidence. Students are often assigned tasks that *require* such skills, but the problem of *acquiring* the requisite skills is left to the ingenuity, good fortune, and native ability of the student.

Furthermore, students are often unaware of the characteristic *forms* in which arguments are presented in different fields. Some disciplines prefer a problem-solution structure; in others, a position on an issue is supported with evidence (Bean and Ramage 1986). Experimental reports in the natural and social sciences favor statement of the problem, hypothesis, methods, findings, and discussion. History is descriptive and narrative at times, interpretive at other times. Many students are only marginally aware of these differences and the reasons for their existence. Moreover, commercial textbooks may obscure the nature and form of disciplinary arguments.

Faculty members' intimate familiarity with the questions and methods of their disciplines would seem to put them in an ideal position to help students acquire the needed skills. Most academics chose their discipline because they had a natural affinity for its ways, however. To them, discipline-specific reasoning skills are second nature. Teaching critical thinking involves making familiar patterns explicit so they can be shared.

Such an enterprise naturally raises many questions. What are the important skills students need to acquire? How do people acquire the skills and dispositions needed to think in the mode of the discipline? How much does thinking depend on specialized knowledge? How much on native ability or affinity for the subject? Does the study of certain subjects foster critical thinking more than others? Does it matter how subjects are taught? Do critical thinking skills learned in one domain transfer to other subjects? While many educators and researchers have explored questions such as these, their findings present a complex and incomplete but comprehensible portrait of critical thinking.

Purpose and Scope of the Report

The purposes of this report are to enrich educators' models of critical thinking and its development and to illustrate how educators have shaped educational settings to nurture the capacity and disposition to think critically. The report examines three major perspectives on critical thinking:

- Informal logic, or critical thinking as skills of analyzing and constructing arguments;
- Cognitive processes, or critical thinking as construction of meaning; and
- Intellectual development, or critical thinking as the manifestation of a contextual theory of knowledge.

Within each perspective, relevant theory and research are reviewed and limitations and educational implications explored.

The report then illustrates current practice in the teaching of critical thinking at two levels: individual courses within a discipline and institutional programs to foster critical thinking. It concludes with recommendations for research and practice and an assessment of prospects for critical thinking as an outcome of higher education.

The perspectives of this report are primarily psychological, educational, and empirical. Other perspectives, however, could certainly enrich such an inquiry—for example, philosophers interested in ethics and values (e.g., Morrill 1980), sociologists interested in the influence of group norms and social structures on reasoning (e.g., Stark 1987), and specialists in communication, rhetoric, and composition who offer important insights on group dynamics, persuasion, and the ways in which language reflects and shapes thinking. Moreover, many educators not discussed here have adapted their teaching practice to cajole, provoke, and entice students into thinking critically. They have a reputation among students, and they offer a rich store of local knowledge for interested colleagues.

Within its psychological perspective, this report does not address motivational issues or learning styles, although it has implications for each of these topics. Two earlier reports in this series address stress in teaching and learning, which has implications for motivation (Whitman, Spendlove, and Clark 1984, 1986); others address learning styles (Claxton and Murrell 1987; Claxton and Ralston 1978). Another book offers a brief overview of affective factors in problem solving (McLeod 1985).

The report maintains a deliberate focus on instruction *in the academic disciplines*. (For a comprehensive review of "generic" thinking skills programs, see Nickerson, Perkins, and Smith 1985.) It presents experimental studies relevant to instruction in the disciplines and theoretically grounded instructional practice supported by documented effects on thinking skills. Many promising courses and programs lack such grounding as yet. For example, this report does not address instruction based on Freire's concepts of education for critical consciousness (1985), although advocates claim powerful effects on students' thinking (see, e.g., Shor 1980, 1987).

Finally, the underlying assumption of the report is one originally articulated by the Soviet psychologist Lev Vygotsky (1978), who observed that children can do more with assistance than they can do unaided. The distance between the two performance levels is a developmental threshold he called the "zone of proximal development": "What a child can do with assistance today she will be able to do by herself tomorrow" (p. 87). This report offers grounds for optimism that students' limitations as critical thinkers can be overcome with the support and guidance of their professors and peers.

HISTORICAL BACKGROUND

The Forerunners
A brief overview of the forerunners and context of the current "movement" sets the stage for discussion of more recent developments.

Dewey
John Dewey stressed the distinction between *process* and *product* in thinking. He defined "reflective thinking" as "active, persistent, and careful consideration of any belief or supposed form of knowledge in the light of the grounds that support it and the further conclusions to which it tends [that] includes a conscious and voluntary effort to establish belief upon a firm basis of evidence and rationality" (1933, p. 9).

Reflective thinking is stimulated by a "perplexed" situation that prompts guesses ("suggestions") about how to resolve it. The rational problem solver pauses to formulate the problem and develop a hypothesis. Observation and reason guide testing and refinement of the hypothesis (1933, pp. 106–15). Like contemporary theorists, Dewey insisted that these processes are not linear but recursive and mutually influential.

Judgment, for Dewey, is reflective thinking turned to controversy; it involves "selecting and weighing the bearing of facts and suggestions as they present themselves, as well as of deciding whether the alleged facts are really facts and whether the idea used is a sound idea or merely a fancy" (pp. 119–20). Dewey observed that learning does not guarantee good judgment; comparing memory to a refrigerator, he states that it provides a "stock of meanings for future use, but judgment selects and adopts the one to be used in an emergency" (p. 125).

Dewey believed that education could either help or hinder development of problem solving and judgment. He advocated education based on the scientific method, capitalizing on students' interests and integrating experience and reflection with learning content (Dewey 1938).

Dewey's ideas stimulated extensive reform rhetoric and were used to justify a reform movement called "progressive education." Progressive education prompted some curricular and instructional changes designed to improve students' thinking skills at the elementary level but resulted in little change in practice in secondary schools (Cuban 1984).

Glaser
A major experiment to test the feasibility of teaching critical thinking to high school students identified three components of

critical thinking: "(1) an attitude of being disposed to consider in a thoughtful way the problems and subjects that come within the range of one's experiences, (2) knowledge of the methods of logical inquiry and reasoning, and (3) some skill in applying those methods" (Glaser 1941, pp. 5–6).

To test the skills of critical thinking, Glaser developed the Watson-Glaser Critical Thinking Appraisal, a multiple-choice test of reasoning skills that is still widely used in studies at the high school and college level (Watson and Glaser 1980; see McMillan 1987 for a review and McPeck 1981 for a critique). The Critical Thinking Appraisal tests skills of arguments, specifically drawing inferences, recognizing assumptions, evaluating conclusions, and assessing the strength of reasons offered in support of a claim.

Glaser's instructional program consisted of eight lessons on topics related to critical thinking, including definition, evidence, inference, scientific method and attitude, prejudice, propaganda, and values and logic. The lessons were taught in English classes over a 10–week period. Following Dewey, Glaser encouraged teachers to capitalize on students' interests in the choice of specific topics for analysis.

Compared with students in four control classes, students in the four experimental classes made significantly greater gains on several subtests of the Watson-Glaser instrument. The study also revealed high correlations between scores for critical thinking and measures of intelligence (.46) and reading comprehension (.77), however, a problem that plagues tests of critical thinking to this day (Facione 1984; McPeck 1981). Students and teachers alike reported satisfaction and enjoyment of the program, and teachers reported seeing many examples of critical thinking on the part of students outside the context of the lessons.

Ennis

Another early and influential view of critical thinking is that of Ennis, coauthor of the Cornell Tests of Critical Thinking Ability (Ennis 1962, 1985, 1986; Ennis and Millman 1985). In his early paper, he defined critical thinking as "the correct assessment of statements"; more recently, he has defined it as "reflective and reasonable thinking that is focused on deciding what to believe or do" (Ennis 1985, p. 45). Ennis's goals for a critical thinking curriculum include "dispositions" (e.g., open-mindedness and staying informed) and abilities like clarifying questions, terms, and assumptions, assessing sources' credibility, reasoning logically, and detecting or using persuasive strategies.

Ennis has published two multiple-choice tests for assessing critical thinking (Ennis and Millman 1985). The college-level test assesses inductive and deductive reasoning, prediction and experimentation, fallacies, definition, and identification of assumptions.

A Piagetian approach

In the late 1950s, Inhelder and Piaget published work describing the development of abstract, systematic, and hypothetical reasoning as evidenced in scientific problem solving (1958). Among the reasoning abilities they identified were separation and control of variables (in their terms, the "schema" of "all other things being equal"), proportional reasoning, hypothetical reasoning, correlational reasoning, and systematic combination of items in a set.

Inhelder and Piaget found that while adolescents could successfully perform tests of these skills, preadolescents could not. They concluded that adolescents use "formal operations," generalized abstract schemas or blueprints that enable them to solve abstract or hypothetical problems independent of their content. Before adolescence, students use "concrete operations," in which reasoning is tied to actual objects or their representations. For example, to combine chemicals in search of a particular reaction, concrete thinkers use trial and error rather than devise a system. When they get a reaction, they stop, failing to consider the possibility that another combination might also produce the reaction. Most concepts taught at the college level require formal thinking.

College and university professors of physics, and later in other disciplines as well, noticed that their students had difficulty performing the kinds of tasks Inhelder and Piaget described. Although Inhelder and Piaget had placed the onset of "formal operations" in early to middle adolescence, researchers in the United States found that large numbers of college freshmen consistently performed concretely on formal tasks (Arons 1976; Lawson and Renner 1974). Such students would be at a disadvantage in college, unless they could rely on rote memory strategies.

This discovery inspired a number of programs and courses designed to help these students develop formal reasoning skills (e.g., Arons 1976; Fuller 1978, 1980; McKinnon 1976). These programs were based on three fundamental Piagetian principles: (1) development is a progression from action-based, concrete "operations" or schemas to abstract, systematized, logical operations; (2) learning is heightened when the learner is surprised by a discrepancy between expectations and real events; and (3) both learning and development require activity on the part of the learner (Piaget 1968). These programs were designed to develop formal reasoning abilities *in conjunction with learning traditional disciplinary "content."* Students in these programs were usually college freshmen, in some cases poorly prepared for college.

An early program to develop formal reasoning, ADAPT, was initiated at the University of Nebraska–Lincoln in 1972 (Fuller 1978, 1980). The program involved several courses organized around a set of reasoning skills, beginning with observation and progressing to systematic control of variables. Participating students enrolled in at least three ADAPT courses so that they learned to use the same reasoning skill in many disciplines at once. All courses in the program used a teaching strategy based on Piaget's three principles, called the "learning cycle" (Karplus 1974, 1977). The learning cycle begins with a concrete "exploration" of a problem designed to raise questions and encourage students to formulate and test hypotheses. In the "concept introduction" phase, students report their findings and formulate concepts. To discourage rote learning, the teacher introduces abstract terminology only when students seem to have grasped underlying concepts. Students extend their understanding in readings, homework assignments, or more advanced classroom activities (the "application" phase).

The ADAPT program enhanced formal reasoning skills and scores on the Watson-Glaser Critical Thinking Appraisal. No comparable gains were found for students in a similarly cohesive program or in a control group of students who had indicated interest in the ADAPT program but were not enrolled in it (Tomlinson-Keasey and Eisert 1978). The ADAPT program is still offered at the University of Nebraska–Lincoln.

Relationship to the Current Scene
Glaser's course description bears many similarities to contemporary critical thinking courses, which emphasize skills of argument, and Ennis's skills approach has been influential in the critical thinking movement in grades K through 12 (see Swartz

1986, e.g.). (Informal logic, an argument skills approach to critical thinking, is described in the next section of this report.)

Two developments in psychology provide the impetus for much of the work reported here. The first is the growth of cognitive science, the interdisciplinary study of human perception, memory, language, learning, and thinking (Gardner 1985). Cognitive researchers share Piaget's belief that human beings *actively construct meaning,* but they differ in their view of the role of knowledge in reasoning. Studies in artificial intelligence (which attempts to simulate human thought processes on computers) have made clear that considerable task-specific knowledge is required to solve even "simple" problems, challenging Piaget's view that abstract logical structures account for reasoning ability. In recent years, teaching methods based on cognitive psychology have been introduced to supplement Piagetian methods (e.g., SOAR at Xavier University—see Carmichael 1982). Dewey's thinking foreshadows cognitive concepts of expert problem solving. Cognitive psychology is the second perspective reviewed in this report.

The second development in psychology was the publication of a study of changes in college students' beliefs about knowledge, truth, and authority (Perry 1970). Perry observed that college experience fosters a gradual recognition of the indeterminacy of knowledge and with that, a recognition of personal responsibility for making judgments and commitments in a relativistic world. He documented this growth among undergraduates at Harvard; more recently, women's intellectual perspectives have also been reported in detail (Belenky et al. 1986). Many educators and researchers have found Perry's model a source of understanding and inspiration for their work; their studies are reviewed in the third section on theory. Reports of course- and institutional-level teaching practices follow these three theoretical reviews.

INFORMAL LOGIC: Analysis and Construction of Arguments

Critical thinking involves the justification of beliefs, and argumentation is the vehicle by which justification is offered. For many people, the term "argument" suggests violent disagreement, or at least a vigorous exchange of ideas. In the context of critical thinking, an argument is a "train of reasoning" in which claims and supporting reasons are linked to establish a position. Arguments are also, however, "human interactions through which such trains of reasoning are formulated, debated, and/or thrashed out" (Toulmin, Rieke, and Janik 1979). Argumentation occurs in various forums or settings—for example, corporate board meetings, engineering design conferences, congressional committee meetings, courts of law (Toulmin, Rieke, and Janik 1979), college classrooms and residence halls, family "councils," town meetings, and many other public and private settings. Further, advertising claims imply arguments, and politicians offer arguments in support of their positions.

Because argumentation is such an important feature of public and private life, achieving skill in constructing and evaluating arguments is a valued educational goal. Most textbooks and courses designed to teach critical thinking aim to develop skill in analyzing arguments, detecting errors in reasoning ("fallacies"), and constructing convincing arguments.

Teaching students to analyze, criticize, and construct arguments offers an appealing resolution to the dilemma of students' deficient reasoning skills. But thinking involves more than argumentation (McPeck 1981; Walters 1986). How justified is the assumption that learning to analyze arguments enhances students' critical thinking ability? To what extent does instruction in the analysis of arguments prepare students for the critical thinking tasks they will face in instruction of subject matter? Should institutions offer introductory courses to teach students general skills of argument? Should instruction in argument be included in general education or specialized discipline-centered courses?

A closer look at what might be included in an introductory course on critical thinking may prove useful in deliberations about these questions. This section provides a brief review and analysis of "informal logic," the approach most often used in textbooks on critical thinking. The section concludes with a discussion of how the study of critical thinking relates to reasoning in courses in the disciplines.

Students can learn the structural features of arguments, but they must also learn the forms and standards of evidence for each field they study.

Rhetoric, Formal Logic, and Informal Logic

Since the time of Aristotle, rhetoricians and logicians have taken as their task the formulation of principles for effective and sound argument. While rhetoric is concerned with persuasiveness of arguments, logic is concerned with the *quality of reasoning* in an argument, that is, with how well it furthers understanding of the subject of inquiry (Beardsley 1975).

Logicians are concerned with the structure of arguments and the ways arguments can go astray. Traditionally, logicians studied deductive and inductive inference using arguments presented in idealized syllogistic forms. In recent years, some logicians have turned to the study of argument as it is practiced in everyday life, or "informal logic" (Johnson and Blair 1980). Teaching "critical thinking," at least at the introductory level, has become almost synonymous with the methods of *applied informal logic.*

Textbooks on critical thinking and courses based on informal logic focus on the structural features of arguments, criteria for evaluation of arguments, and the fallacies or sources of error that can make an argument *seem* valid when it is not (Girle 1983; Johnson and Blair 1980; McPeck 1981). Several key concepts, defined below, are found in such texts.

Types of Arguments

Formal arguments are deductive; their conclusions follow necessarily from their premises. The familiar syllogism is the prototype:

(premise)   1. If A, then B.
(premise)   2. A; therefore,
(conclusion) 3. B.

Or, in more concrete terms:

1. If the president doesn't act forcefully, he'll lose points in the polls.
2. He won't act forcefully; therefore,
3. He'll lose points in the polls (Kahane 1984, p. 8).

Informal arguments are inductive; inductive arguments involve making generalizations rather than drawing firm conclusions. Their conclusions can only be more or less probable; they can never be established as absolutely true. The premises used in such arguments can be based on causality, analogy, comparisons, or statistics (Kahane 1984; Kelly 1988). For example, *U.S. presidents are unlikely to act forcefully because they fear a loss of popularity in public opinion polls,* where the premise is that U.S. presidents fear a loss of popularity in the opinion polls and the conclusion is that U.S. presidents are unlikely to act forcefully. But an additional premise is implied: *U.S. presidents' actions are guided by the reactions they anticipate in the polls.* Missing premises (or "enthymemes") must be inferred for the argument to make sense (Boylan 1988; Kelly 1988). Often (as in the examples given here), they contain key assumptions that must be questioned.

A *cogent* argument rests on premises that are justified or warranted; its reasoning is valid—that is, no fallacies or errors of inference are involved—and, if it is inductive, it uses all available information relevant to the subject (Kahane 1980). Most arguments are the informal, inductive type.

The probabilistic nature of informal arguments means that they must be developed, that is, additional premises supplied, to be convincing (Johnson and Blair 1980). Developing informal arguments requires a store of relevant knowledge, flexible thinking, and ingenuity, as many different kinds of premises may be brought to bear on the issue. Informal arguments are dialectical; that is, reasoners "interrogate" their knowledge base in search of possible objections or counterarguments. Consequently, new premises can be brought in to challenge previous statements, often causing a change in the reasoner's idea (or "model") of the situation. Premises may also be abandoned when a flaw or competing alternative is discovered. In an informal argument, even a well-supported conclusion can be questioned (Perkins, Allen, and Hafner 1983).

Fallacies of Informal Reasoning
The complex, dynamic quality of informal arguments renders them particularly susceptible to faulty reasoning. Philosophers (and also psychologists) have identified numerous errors in reasoning (see Kahneman, Slovic, and Tversky 1982 for an impressive catalog of studies on this subject). Philosophers refer to these errors as "fallacies." Descriptions and examples of fallacies abound in textbooks on critical thinking. For example:

1. *Provincialism:* The tendency to accept or reject ideas on the basis of experience in one's own group or society

rather than on evidence or in light of knowledge and beliefs of other societies.

2. *Ad hominem:* An attack on a person's credibility or character rather than on the arguments presented.

3. *False dilemma:* "Erroneously reducing the number of possible choices on an issue" (Barry 1983, p. 108). Questionnaires frequently create false dilemmas; writing assignments that ask students to defend a position on an issue may similarly restrict thinking.

4. *Hasty conclusion or generalization:* Drawing conclusions from too little evidence or from unrepresentative samples.

5. *Begging the question, circularity:* "Endorsing without proof some form of the very question at issue" (Kahane 1984, p. 82) (Barry 1983; Kahane 1984; Toulmin, Rieke, and Janik 1979).

Other fallacies commonly mentioned are straw men, suppressed evidence, non sequiturs or "irrelevant reason" (Kahane 1980), appeal to authority, arguing from what is to what ought to be, wishful thinking, and self-deception.

Critical Thinking Textbooks

A brief look at several current textbooks for courses on critical thinking reveals a shared focus on reasoning as "a way of testing ideas critically" (Toulmin, Rieke, and Janik 1979, p. 9). All provide instruction and practice exercises in the analysis of arguments and identification of fallacies in reasoning. Most authors have abandoned Latin terminology in favor of English names for arguments and fallacies (Johnson and Blair 1980). Beyond these common starting points, texts vary on several dimensions:

1. The relative importance they assign to fallacy and to analysis of argument structure;

2. Their emphasis on technical features of arguments, for example, details of inductive and deductive reasoning, or application of a particular analytical format;

3. The kinds of examples they use: short or extended, actual or invented arguments, visual as well as verbal presentations, and use of examples from the popular media;

4. The style of the author, ranging from friendly and concrete to authoritative and formal;

5. The relative emphasis on analyzing versus constructing arguments.

Texts that stress analysis of arguments include Boylan's *The Process of Argument* (1988), Browne and Keeley's *Asking the Right Questions* (1986), and Toulmin, Rieke, and Janik's *An Introduction to Reasoning* (1979). Boylan describes a method for outlining arguments to reveal their central premises and controversial points. He demonstrates the method on inductive and pictoral arguments, using both invented and actual examples, but discusses evaluation of arguments and fallacy only briefly. Browne and Keeley identify 12 questions to ask in evaluating an argument. Several extended examples are taken from the popular press, for example, articles on the 55-mph speed limit and licensing parents; others are invented. Toulmin, Rieke, and Janik present a model for analysis of arguments and illustrate its use in fields ranging from football to ethics. The text illustrates the model's application and discusses issues of argumentation in law, science, art, management, and ethics. Exercises include examples from popular media; for example, the chapter on conclusions provides extensive comparative data on four compact automobiles from *Consumer Reports*, while the chapter on reasoning in the arts uses a review of a record album from *Rolling Stone*.

The Art of Reasoning offers a conceptual approach (Kelly 1988). The author begins with chapters on concepts, definitions, and propositions, using diagrams to outline a structure of argument. He then describes inductive and deductive arguments and illustrates them in depth; separate chapters are devoted to fallacy, analogy, causality, and statistics. Exercises include examples from many sources. Copi's text, *Informal Logic* (1986), also takes a conceptual approach, with chapters on language, reasoning by analogy, and definition. It emphasizes causality and scientific reasoning and includes an extended analysis of John Stuart Mill's method. Copi uses a graphic system for diagramming arguments; his examples are drawn from diverse sources, including historical and philosophical texts and the Bible. Beardsley's *Thinking Straight* (1975) is also conceptual, with emphasis on the structure of deductive arguments and various forms of inductive reasoning. He includes chapters on the "pitfalls" and "resources" of language in arguments, with attention to ambiguity, vagueness, emotive language, metaphor, and slant, and discusses fallacies throughout the text. Examples are drawn from news media or invented based on actual issues.

Fallacy is the central focus in Kahane's *Logic and Contemporary Rhetoric* (1984). The text is replete with examples from many sources that illustrate how self-deception and wishful thinking prevent critical evaluation of ideas and permit inaccurate or inconsistent world views to persist. Language, advertising, extended arguments, news media, and textbooks are closely analyzed in terms of the world views they present. Techniques for analyzing and constructing arguments are introduced in a single chapter midway through the text.

Three texts exemplify approaches that integrate reasoning and writing. The authors share the view that teaching critical reading and thinking must be supplemented with instruction in argumentative writing. Gage's *The Shape of Reason: Argumentative Writing in College* (1987) is holistic rather than analytical in approach. The task Gage addresses is formulating a position through critical reading and inquiry, then setting forth reasons for one's conclusions, as opposed to argumentation as an effort to win a case by persuasion. The text emphasizes responsible decision making in reading, developing a point of view, finding support for it, and presenting it (and oneself) in writing. Examples are invented (or possibly drawn from students' work). Barry, in *Good Reason for Writing* (1983), treats both principles of argument and methods for composing arguments. He presents four rhetorical patterns commonly used in argumentative writing: the opinion essay, essays of comparison or analogy, cause-and-effect essays, and extended definition. A chapter on troubleshooting discusses more than 50 common fallacies, with examples drawn from numerous sources. Bean and Ramage (1986) also describe rhetorical patterns; they offer a composition text grounded in argumentation and supported by extensive guidance in formulating questions and thinking dialectically during the phase of discovery.

Ruggierio's *The Art of Thinking: A Guide to Critical and Creative Thought* (1984) also emphasizes discovery and development of ideas. He offers ways to broaden perspectives, rekindle curiosity, sharpen analytical skills, and become more creative. The text walks the student through several phases of thinking, beginning with creative processes involved in identifying and investigating problems and generating possible solutions. The author demonstrates the role of criticism in developing ideas and encourages students to anticipate negative reactions so they can build a persuasive case. Appendixes briefly summarize fundamentals of composition and logic.

Of these texts, Barry, Ruggierio, Kahane, and Bean and Ramage most consistently suggest exercises that involve composing original arguments. The remaining texts focus primarily on practicing analytical methods.

Transferable Aspects of Argument

The origins of critical thinking texts in informal logic clarify why analysis and construction of arguments are prominent features in such texts. A fundamental question that remains, however, is the degree to which learning the skills of argument enables students to reason effectively in various disciplines.

McPeck (1981) argues that critical thinking is discipline specific because it depends on knowledge of what constitutes good reasons in a discipline, which requires extensive knowledge of the subject matter. He concludes that critical thinking is not a generalized skill and that instruction in critical thinking without a solid foundation of specialized knowledge tends to "underestimate and play down the real complexities that usually underlie even apparently 'common' or 'everyday' problems" (p. 156).

How this question is answered rests in part on an assessment of the degree to which arguments share common features across disciplines. Toulmin's influential analysis (1958) identifies six basic elements found in arguments on any subject, in any field. He calls the conclusion in traditional terminology a *claim*; the premises become *data* or grounds on which the claim rests. The relationship between the claim and the data is expressed in a *warrant,* which is often an unstated premise (as in the presidential argument above). *Backing* is often needed to justify the warrant in an informal argument. In addition, the *modality* of the argument is expressed in qualifiers that indicate the force with which the claim is asserted. The argument may also contain a *rebuttal*, or statement of exceptions or conditions under which the warrant might not hold true.

These common elements make it clear that fields use different kinds of backing to justify warrants (e.g., statutes for legal claims, statistical information for claims about the distribution of phenomena) as well as kinds of evidence to support claims and criteria used to evaluate evidence. Toulmin concludes that arguments cannot be measured against any universal or formal standard; they must be evaluated against "whatever sort of cogency or well-foundedness can relevantly be asked for *in that field*" (p. 248, emphasis added).

Thus, students can learn the structural features of arguments, but they must also learn the forms and standards of evidence for each field they study. This view guides the essentially discipline-based organization of Toulmin's recent text on reasoning (Toulmin, Rieke, and Janik 1979). The model has also been used to teach argumentative writing (Bean and Ramage 1986) and beginning speech (Verderber 1967). Discipline-specific argument skills have been taught in an introductory psychology course using Toulmin's model (Cerbin 1988), and the model has been used in research on problem solving in the social sciences (Voss, Tyler, and Yengo 1983).

Many authors have proposed inventories of argument skills (e.g., Arons 1985; Ennis 1985, 1986; Nickerson 1986c). All would agree that background knowledge of a topic is essential to good argument. Moreover, acquiring skills in the methodology of a field takes years of study. High expectations for critical thinking among undergraduates may therefore be unrealistic (Facione 1984). Nevertheless, instruction can help students learn to determine "which data to attend to, and how to organize these data to maximize their implications" (p. 261). Essential skills include:

1. *Identifying issues requiring the application of thinking skills informed by background knowledge;*
2. *Determining the nature of the background knowledge that is relevant to deciding the issues involved and gathering that knowledge;*
3. *Generating initially plausible hypotheses regarding the issues;*
4. *Developing procedures to test these hypotheses, which procedures lead to the confirmation or disconfirmation of those hypotheses;*
5. *Articulating in argument form the results of these testing procedures; and*
6. *Evaluating . . . arguments and, where appropriate, revising the initial hypotheses in the light of alternative understandings developed during the testing process* (Facione 1984, p. 261; see also Facione 1986, p. 226).

This approach is illustrated in a reading course (Stasz and

Associates 1985). Students learn to explore a problem or topic by identifying what they already know about it and what more they need to know *before* they begin reading to gather information about it. The statement of the problem and the solution emerge from their inquiry. This approach is applicable in many disciplines; at the same time, the questions that arise from particular explorations invite discussion of criteria for evaluating evidence in context.

Thus, although McPeck demonstrates limitations of several current attempts to identify and teach common skills of argument, his "discipline-specific approach obscures the commonalities evident across disciplines" (Facione 1986, p. 226).

Critique of Critical Thinking as Analysis of Arguments
Informal logic as an approach to critical thinking has been criticized on several grounds.

Critical thinking courses teach skills but do not challenge thinking. One author argues that critical thinking courses encourage sophistry by teaching students skills they can then use to rationalize their existing biases (Paul 1982, 1986). Alternatively, students who discover that any position can be defended may dismiss the entire process, preferring to rely on intuition or feelings. In either case, by emphasizing analysis and "correction" of fallacies, these courses miss the point that irrationality is a fundamental human characteristic, inherent in the way "world views"—complex networks of beliefs and knowledge—are constructed and protected. Paul (1986) advocates teaching critical thinking in the "strong" sense—"teaching it so that students explicate, understand, and critique their own deepest prejudices, biases, and misconceptions, thereby allowing [them] to discover and contest their own egocentric and sociocentric tendencies" (p. 140). He deliberately selects complex issues that students care about and that "engage their egocentric thoughts and beliefs" (p. 140), then fosters "dialogical" thinking about the issues by insisting that students "argue for and against . . . every important point of view and each basic belief or conclusion that they are to take seriously" (p. 140). An earlier article describes a critical thinking course in which students confront their nationalistic biases (Paul 1982).

Paul's claim is that critical thinking courses fail to address the fundamental weakness in people's reasoning, their tendency to maintain existing beliefs. As noted in the introduction, researchers have generally found that beliefs are extremely resistant to change. Emphasizing analytical skills may improve students' ability to justify beliefs they already hold without significantly improving their disposition to weigh evidence objectively.

Courses that address controversial issues directly may be more successful in this regard. In at least one documented instance, however, students classified as authoritarian became more polarized in their views on a controversial topic (racial integration of housing in the 1950s) as a result of instruction in critical thinking (Stern and Cope 1956). Students' responses to critical thinking courses reflect their assumptions about the truth, knowledge, and authority and their awareness of contextual influences on judgment. Different assumptions may require different forms of instruction. Theories of intellectual development, taken up in a later section of this report, address this interpretation.

Critical thinking courses misrepresent thinking. Critical thinking courses that emphasize "analytical reductionism" may leave students with the impression that "critical" thinking is the *only* valid form of thought (Walters 1986). They may devalue other forms, such as aesthetic or contemplative thought, if they are not given equal weight in the curriculum. McPeck (1981) goes one step farther, questioning the assumption that these courses even teach "critical thinking." They teach *analysis of arguments,* which is a logician's craft and may have little to do with critical thinking. For example, they emphasize the "context of justification" but neglect the "context of discovery," which is the source of both hypotheses and alternatives in real-world reasoning. Discovery is viewed as the "domain of psychologists" (Kahane 1980, p. 37).

Critical thinking courses can have several possible negative outcomes (Girle 1983). First, they convey the view that even the best argument can be criticized; second, analysis of truncated arguments implies that context, development, and nuance are unimportant in arguments. Further, when students only criticize and are not responsible for producing alternatives, they are not learning to reason, only to analyze the reasoning of others. And by taking as their object of study "set pieces," or arguments taken out of context and prepared for analysis, such courses fail to convey that argumentation is a *dialogue* in which "good argument can be vindicated, poor argument revealed, opinions changed, and the search for truth can proceed" (Girle 1983, p. 146).

The value of critical thinking courses is not supported by empirical evidence. Several investigators have noted the shortage of empirical evidence that such courses positively influence students' reasoning in subsequent courses. They have also noted, however, that anecdotal reports of the benefits of such courses are frequent and that students' and instructors' satisfaction with them is often quite high (Nickerson, Perkins, and Smith 1985; Resnick 1987). Some precollegiate programs have been evaluated, and the results are generally positive (e.g., Glaser 1941; Herrnstein et al. 1986). Evaluation of four separate sections of one course revealed that students improved on several aspects of argument analysis. But exhaustive analysis frustrated their understanding of the issue as a whole (Bernstein and Brouwer 1986). More such studies are needed.

Educational Implications

What might instruction in critical thinking contribute to reasoning in the disciplines?

McPeck's argument against "generic" courses in critical thinking skills rests in part on the claim that analysis of arguments is not central to reasoning in the disciplines. The reasoning processes of disciplinary experts often depend on tacit knowledge that may need to be made explicit for beginners, however. Courses in critical thinking foster explicitness about reasoning by focusing students' attention on analytic processes and by providing experience in reasoning at a level appropriate to their abilities.

A college-level course in critical thinking is probably the first opportunity most students have had to focus attention on their own reasoning processes. Engaging in relatively superficial arguments in various subjects sensitizes students to the diversity, if not the complexity, of arguments. At the same time, it provides concrete experience in recognizing the common elements of arguments. Such experience helps them develop their understanding of what an argument is. As novices in the academic world, students, especially freshmen, will not produce extended arguments for quite some time. Therefore, although courses in critical thinking may not demand extended arguments or employ sophisticated criteria for evaluating arguments, they offer practice at a level that is compatible with students' initial entry into the field of argument.

Analysis of arguments also provides practice in academically important skills like reading comprehension, summarization, analysis, comparison and contrast, and evaluation of ideas. Similar skills are frequently the focus of programs to improve reading and study habits, many of which have had documented success. By making students aware of the ways in which arguments can be organized, courses in critical thinking attune them to the structure and logic of texts. Similarly, identification of fallacies encourages close reading of texts, something students may never have done.

Most important, courses on thinking provide opportunities for discussion of ideas with other students. Controversy compels students to confront their biases and may stimulate them to rethink their ideas, either to find new justifications or to revise them in the light of better arguments. Attitudes and beliefs about controversial issues are highly resistant to change, but they are unlikely to change at all if they are not challenged in some disciplined and ultimately supportive manner.

This analysis is based on the assumption that students will in fact practice using the skills of argument presented in texts on critical thinking. Some texts clearly lend themselves to practical application more than others, and professors may differ in the degree to which they emphasize application as opposed to concepts. In planning courses to teach thinking, students' level of involvement in class discussion and opportunities for practice and feedback on skills are as important as decisions about how many credits the course should be worth, who will teach the course, and what textbook (if any) will be used.

The most fundamental limitation of courses in critical thinking skills is that the questions we ask determine the value of our inquiry, and, without knowledge of the subject of inquiry, it is difficult to ask intelligent questions. For this reason, introductory courses on thinking cannot substitute for discipline-based instruction in reasoning. They do offer one avenue for initiating students into the complexities and challenges of reasoning they will encounter in subsequent courses, however. This initiation must be reinforced and extended in disciplinary study.

The next section examines relationships between subject knowledge and reasoning skill in greater detail.

COGNITIVE PROCESSES IN CRITICAL THINKING

Informal logic clarifies the forms arguments can take and provides guidance in identifying fallacious arguments. It illuminates the *context of justification,* the phase of argument in which conclusions are set forth and supported once they have been reached. Left unexplored are questions of how people arrive at conclusions, how knowledge influences reasoning processes, how people learn to use the methods of specific disciplines to address complex issues, and how they direct and sustain attention to the demanding, multifaceted task of thinking critically. Most perplexing, while logicians generate ever-expanding lists of fallacies in reasoning, their lists provide little help in understanding *why* people persist in reasoning erroneously, even when they have been alerted to the dangers of fallacious reasoning.

Cognitive research does not address all the questions left unanswered by logicians. It does, however, provide educators with a window on students' reasoning processes and how they influence students' academic work. Thus, cognitive research is relevant to the *context of discovery.* After a brief summary of assumptions, this section reviews research on reasoning processes in several disciplines. The research reveals the extent and nature of the gap between beginning and advanced (student and faculty) thinkers. The last part of this section analyzes research on instructional strategies designed to close that gap.

The process of developing support for a position most clearly distinguishes critical thinking from problem solving.

Assumptions

The study of cognition has become an interdisciplinary field encompassing linguistics, anthropology, artificial intelligence, philosophy, psychology, and education (Gardner 1985; Stevens and Gentner 1983). To say that such a diverse research community shares many assumptions risks making a statement so broad as to be meaningless. Several themes relevant to instruction for critical thinking can be detected in the work of researchers in this field, however.

A person is *not a tabula rasa.* The "cognitive revolution" in psychology views perception, learning, understanding, and problem solving as purposeful behavior whose function is to give meaning to experience by imposing order upon it.

Because we lack the cognitive capacities to apprehend the world as it is, we are forced to construct representations of that world and to engage in thinking and reasoning within the confines of those constructions . . . . Individuals actively make use of cognitive strategies and previous knowledge to deal with their cognitive limitations (Shulman and Carey 1984, pp. 508, 509, emphasis added).

Given a problem, story, event, work of art, or phenomenon of any sort, people interpret or *represent* it in terms of what they already know or believe. They are not "blank slates" upon which information can be written or "reality" faithfully copied. In fact, their existing beliefs are so powerful that they can inhibit learning of concepts that do not "fit." For example, people do not retell unconventional stories as they hear them but reconstruct them to conform to their experiences and expectations (Bartlett 1932).

Knowledge is meaningful information stored in memory. To make its way into memory, knowledge must be acted upon by the learner. In terms of the metaphor of information processing that dominates cognitive psychology, *short-term memory* is the active processing function that translates stimulation into familiar terms so that it becomes "information." Information that the learner integrates with prior learning becomes usable "knowledge," which is stored in *long-term memory*. But as noted earlier, information is not stored exactly as it is presented; what is stored is *meaning,* as constructed by the learner. In terms of classroom learning, this model implies that students remember *what they understand,* not necessarily what is said.

Knowledge in memory is organized. When people encounter familiar subjects, their prior knowledge enables them to distinguish important from unimportant aspects of the situation. Their knowledge is organized into patterns that provide a context for new information, which are called "scripts" (Schank and Abelson 1977) or "schemas" (Anderson 1985; Bartlett 1932; Rumelhart 1977). When people do not have an appropriate schema for a situation, they have difficulty remembering information about it. For example, in a study of people's recollection of information from a story about a baseball game, baseball fans remembered numerous details, especially events related to scoring. People unfamiliar with the game remembered little of this information but picked up details about familiar elements, such as the weather (Spilich et al. 1979). Students taking a course in an unfamiliar subject suffer the same disadvantage as "baseball illiterates" reading about a baseball game.

Expertise results from gradual development of high-level schemas that enable experts to quickly recognize and categorize frequently recurring patterns of information in their field, called "chunks." For a physician a cluster of symptoms is a chunk, for a musician a cluster of notes from a familiar work, for a scholar key terms and names of leading thinkers in the field. Chunks enable experts to scan a research paper or book or glance at an artifact and quickly develop a hypothesis as to its theoretical orientation or origin. Experts call upon a working vocabulary estimated at 50,000 chunks. These chunks serve as an "index" to the many schemas that organize experts' knowledge in their field (Simon 1980). Novices have few such patterns; hence, their problem-solving processes are slower and less effective. At the normal rate of learning, it takes about 10 years to become an "expert" (Simon 1980).

In the classroom, students benefit from instruction that helps them organize what they are learning, for example, into a matrix or hierarchy. Hierarchies that clarify cause-and-effect relationships are especially helpful (Armbruster 1984). A student can begin immediately to construct a schema for an unfamiliar topic from a causally structured outline.

Knowledge takes many forms. Reasoning about any subject calls upon several forms of knowledge. One form, *declarative knowledge,* includes concepts, principles, stories, and other proposition knowledge that is used to make inferences. Second, the learner must know how and when to use declarative knowledge to execute a skilled performance. This aspect of knowledge, called *procedural* or *strategic knowledge,* describes what a person can *do* (Anderson 1985; Greeno 1980). Examples include knowing how to drive a car, find information in the library, or write a book review.

Competent problem solvers also plan and monitor their work using executive control strategies. They make plans, set goals and subgoals, ask questions, take notes, observe the effectiveness of their efforts, and take corrective action when necessary. In problem solving, metacognition directs attention to the knowledge base in search of information relevant to the problem. *Metacognition* is a term frequently used to refer to control strategies (Flavell 1976, 1979).

Two important principles relevant to instruction for critical thinking follow from the assumption of multiple forms of knowledge:

1. Declarative knowledge alone is necessary but not sufficient for development of skilled performance. Students must also learn strategies or procedures for using their knowledge and conditions under which specific knowledge is relevant (Bransford et al. 1986; Perfetto, Bransford, and Franks 1983; Simon 1980).
2. While some general strategies for problem solving may exist, skill in solving most problems depends a great deal on the extent and organization of the knowledge base available to the problem solver (Larkin, Heller, and Greeno 1980; Simon 1980).

Critical Thinking as Problem Solving

Critical thinking is a form of problem solving, but a major difference between the two is that critical thinking involves reasoning about open-ended or "ill-structured" problems, while problem solving is usually considered narrower in scope. The primary difference, however, lies in what happens after a conclusion (solution, hypothesis) is reached. Problem solving has been well studied by cognitive scientists, although critical thinking has not.

Problem solving is mental activity leading from an unsatisfactory state to a more desired "goal state." As in critical thinking, problem solvers construct and then refine a "model" of the problematic situation. They analyze their current state, identify constraints, gather information, generate one or more hypotheses, and test their hypotheses until the goal is achieved (Anderson 1985; Newell and Simon 1972).

In problem solving as studied in cognition laboratories, the problems are often complex but a correct answer usually exists, and only a limited number of approaches (possibly only one) will work. Such problems are often referred to as "well structured." In contrast, critical thinking involves inductive reasoning, or reasoning about "ill-structured problems" that have no single solution. Thus, in critical thinking, the goal is not to find and execute a solution but to construct a *plausible representation of the situation or issue that could be presented in a convincing argument.*

The representation (or "situation model"—Perkins, Allen, and Hafner 1983) can be summarized in the form of a proposition or "claim" that purports to account for all available information. Whether the claim is an interpretation of a literary or artistic work, a position on a controversial issue, or a proposal for the solution of a complex problem, it cannot be proven or tested; hence, it must be *supported* with appropriate reasoning and evidence (Voss, Tyler, and Yengo 1983). The process of developing support for a position most clearly distinguishes critical thinking from problem solving.

Many resources are candidates for inclusion in reasoning about ill-defined problems (Perkins 1986). For example, political science experts were asked how they would solve the problem of improving agricultural production in the Soviet Union. The causes they identified, and hence the solutions they proposed, differed widely (Voss, Greene, Post, and Penner 1983; Voss, Tyler, and Yengo 1983). Despite their shared discipline, they applied very different "scripts" to the problem. In comparison to physics or mathematics, the particular knowledge base of the problem solver appears to be a more salient factor in social science problems (Voss, Greene, Post, and Penner 1983) and probably in other less consensual fields as well.

The apparent difference between critical thinking (associated with the social sciences and humanities) and problem solving (associated with mathematics and physics) may be an artifact of the problems used in cognitive research. Studies of problem solving use well-structured (though nontrivial) problems, but when physicists and mathematicians conduct research, the problems they face are naturally more open ended. Notes from the research of the physicist Michael Faraday reveal that his research strategy was similar to that of social scientists addressing ill-structured problems. His experiments explored two hypotheses and were designed to develop lines of argumentation (Tweeney 1981, cited in Voss, Greene, Post, and Penner 1983). Furthermore, the scope of an apparently well-defined problem can—and often should—be extended, as in the case of an engineering problem whose solution has real-world implications (Simon and Simon 1979).

Reasoning in the professions, e.g., business, engineering, teaching, or architecture, combines characteristics of both problem solving and critical thinking. In professional practice, problems are ill defined, but solutions can often be tested, although without scientific or mathematical precision. Faced with complex problems, professionals conduct informal but rigorous "action experiments," evaluate the results of their experiments, and modify their approaches based on the results (Argyris, Putnam, and Smith 1985; Schon 1983, 1987). Action experiments allow practitioners to act with some assurance even when problems are ill defined. Their hypothesis-testing quality allows the practitioner to learn from the outcomes.

Thus, although critical thinking and problem solving differ in important ways, the overlap between them is substantial enough to justify close examination of problem solving and related processes for insight regarding critical thinking.

Reasoning of Novices and Experts

Educators often express dismay at the poor quality of reasoning students use to solve problems or think critically about topics presented in their courses. They may believe that they have little control over the quality of work their students produce. How do problem-solving abilities develop? What factors differentiate effective from ineffective reasoners? And what, if anything, can faculty do to enhance their students' performance in reasoning?

Cognitive studies often compare the reasoning processes of novices or inexperienced problem solvers (usually undergraduates in introductory courses) with those of experts or effective problem solvers (Bloom and Broder 1950; Chase and Simon 1973; Faigley and Witte 1981; Flower and Hayes 1980; Larkin et al. 1980; Newell and Simon 1972; Schoenfeld 1983a, 1985a, 1985b; Sommers 1980; Voss, Greene, Post, and Penner 1983; Voss, Tyler, and Yengo 1983). These studies frequently employ a method first used by Duncker (1945), in which the problem solver is asked to report all thoughts while completing a task. Protocols from think-aloud studies provide a data base from which researchers have induced patterns of behavior and organization of knowledge associated with the performance of complex cognitive tasks. Their findings help to understand students' difficulties in the early stages of learning a discipline.

Novices and experts differ in their use of declarative, procedural, and metacognitive knowledge. In addition, some researchers have noted the influence of beliefs about the nature of the task (Ryan 1984a, 1984b; Schoenfeld 1983a, 1985a, 1985b). A few cognitive theorists have also noted the importance of affective, dispositional, and situational factors, such as purpose (Perkins 1981), intrinsic motivation (Malone 1981), determination (Polya 1957), and emotion (McLeod 1985; see also Nickerson, Perkins, and Smith 1985).

Novice-expert studies reveal striking differences between the two groups and striking similarities within groups, regardless of discipline. For example, experts work at the level of principles and plans before plunging into the intricate details of a solution. They may explore a number of possible representations of a problem before they commit to a particular solution. Echoing Dewey's (1933) phenomenological description of reflective thinking, experts treat a solution plan as a hypothesis, checking their progress frequently to avoid a "wild goose chase" (Schoenfeld 1985b, p. 366). Experts also use heuristics to advance understanding of the problem. Successful problem solvers aggressively seek connections between the present problem and what they already know (Greenfield 1987). Novices, in contrast, exhibit tendencies that preclude success, such as categorizing the problem on the basis of superficial features (Chi, Feltovich, and Glaser 1981), failing to include all elements of the problem in their representation, using trial and error instead of analysis (Schoenfeld 1985a, 1985b), and quitting (Bloom and Broder 1950).

The following paragraphs illustrate these differences for problem solving in mathematics, composition, reading comprehension, physics, art history, and political science.

Mathematics
Expert problem solvers read the problem, analyze it, explore it if necessary in search of relevant information, plan, implement, and verify the solution. They monitor the effectiveness of their efforts continually (Schoenfeld 1985a).

Novices exhibit similar processes, but the proportion of time they devote to each differs radically from the pattern observed for experts. Experts spend more time in analysis and planning, while novices tend to advance rapidly toward implementation. Novices pay attention to form rather than to meaning, in one case spending more time "copying over" a proof than they spent developing it (Schoenfeld 1985a).

Composition
Studies of cognitive processes in writing yield very similar patterns, although the context and terminology differ. The problem is to compose an essay that meets the needs of the writer as well as a given audience. Expert writers study the rhetorical situation and develop a detailed representation of their audience, their aims, their presentation of self, and the text. Novices focus on the topic, giving scant attention to the problems of communicating with an audience (Flower and Hayes 1980). When revising, expert writers and advanced students freely alter the

meaning of their original texts. Inexperienced writers are timid, making primarily surface changes; they rarely change meanings (Faigley and Witte 1981). For beginners, the text is a solution, not a hypothesis. Once advanced, it is not subject to significant review or revision. Beginners may detect problems in a text but be unable to diagnose and correct them (Flower et al. 1986).

Reading comprehension

Reading is not simply a matter of absorbing individual words; rather, it is a progressive effort to construct a "model of the meaning of the text" (Armbruster 1984). Effective readers remain absorbed by texts until a triggering event, such as a pile-up of poorly understood words, signals a failure to understand what they are reading. They then decide what action to take to correct the situation so that they can continue reading. In contrast, poor readers often do not recognize their own failure to understand a word or passage they are reading and so are unable to correct the situation (Palincsar and Brown 1984).

Physics

Physics experts represent problems in terms of the laws or principles needed to solve them, e.g., energy equations or Newton's laws of motion. Lacking a scientific understanding of these principles, novices categorize problems on the basis of superficial features, such as whether they involve pulleys, inclined planes, or other objects (Chi, Feltovich, and Glaser 1981; Larkin, Heller, and Greeno 1980; Larkin and Reif 1979).

Art history

To "solve the problem" of understanding a painting, both novices and experts attend to formal elements of paintings (color, line, perspective), particularly when faced with an abstract work. Novices respond to representational works in terms of semantic content ("story") and mood, categories that experts use less often. In contrast, experts synthesize their observations and subordinate them in terms of categories, such as symbolism or the artist's intentions. They support their interpretations with visual evidence from the painting (Schmidt, McLaughlin, and Leighten n.d.).

Political science

Expert political scientists use more abstract categories than novices to identify the causes of problems; graduate students in political science are intermediate in their level of abstractness in citing causes. Experts use different strategies, preferring to identify and eliminate causes in light of political or other constraints, while novices simply start listing solutions. Completion of a single course on the subject has no noticeable effect on undergraduates' representation of the problem; it does, however, slightly increase the complexity of the arguments they use to support their claims (Voss, Greene, Post, and Penner 1983; Voss, Tyler, and Yengo 1983).

Limitations
Expert-novice comparison studies suffer several limitations. First, they are based on laboratory studies of individuals working in an artificial situation (talking out loud while solving complex problems or, in some cases, problem solving in pairs). The sample sizes in many cases are small, and individual differences are present (e.g., Voss, Greene, Post, and Penner 1983; Voss, Tyler, and Yengo 1983). Furthermore, novices are unlikely to have the degree of aptitude for the subject observed in those who go on to become experts, so study participants are not on a developmental continuum (Schoenfeld and Herrmann 1982). Moreover, the fact that experts use certain strategies is no guarantee that teaching those strategies to students will improve their performance; in fact, to the degree that strategies depend on background knowledge, novices may have difficulty using them at all. Evidence reviewed below, however, suggests that instruction based on inferences from these and related studies can improve students' problem solving.

Acquiring Knowledge for Critical Thinking
Students often fail to use knowledge from their courses to analyze new problems. Two, perhaps three, courses taught by traditional methods may be necessary to influence students' use of knowledge and discipline-specific reasoning strategies (Nisbett et al. 1987; Voss et al. 1986). This section reviews studies with implications for accelerating development of students' abilities in critical thinking and problem solving in discipline-based instruction.

Declarative knowledge
Acquiring large amounts of information does not ensure that it will be used in subsequent reasoning (Bransford et al. 1986; Perkins 1986; Perfetto, Bransford, and Franks 1983; Voss et

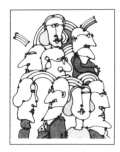

al. 1986; Voss, Greene, Post, and Penner 1983). Declarative knowledge can be acquired through memorization, but knowledge acquired by rote is not helpful in solving unfamiliar problems or thinking about complex issues (Collins, Brown, and Newman 1986). Knowledge must be well understood—reconstructed in schemas in memory—to be useful to the learner. It must also be *organized* and *accessible* to the learner.

Understanding. Students' success as problem solvers is often hampered by limited or incorrect understanding of concepts needed to construct an adequate model of the problem. Students often hold intuitive conceptions or misconceptions that persist even after college-level instruction (Carey 1986; Clement 1983; diSessa 1983). Misconceptions are "consistent ideas reliably held by the reasoner, which differ from scientific conceptions held by experts" (Linn 1986, p. 167). For example, even after a year of college physics, many novices hold the non-Newtonian view that an upward force is exerted on an object when it is tossed into the air; gravity is acting on it only on the way down (Clement 1983). Misconceptions can be observed in other domains as well. For example, the widespread belief in creationism presents instructional challenges equivalent to those of restructuring knowledge in physics. Like scientific theories, misconceptions are not relinquished easily. If misconceptions are present, the learner must do more than acquire information. Knowledge may have to be restructured, with new conceptions replacing old ones, for true understanding to occur (Carey 1986; Linn 1986; Vosniadou and Brewer 1987).

The persistence of misconceptions after instruction is evidence that present instructional methods fail to counteract students' prior understanding of the subject. Misconceptions become apparent when students make predictions based on their schemas, then test their predictions against actual events. Piagetian methods described earlier employ this strategy, as do inquiry methods, described later. Galileo used a similar method to persuade his colleagues that Aristotelian concepts were incorrect (diSessa 1983). Analogies, metaphors, and physical models are also important (Vosniadou and Brewer 1987). Dialogue and physical models can be effective even without significant guidance by a teacher, as illustrated in a transcript of two college students figuring out the balance beam (Lochhead 1979).

Much of the declarative knowledge students must acquire can

be cast in terms of cause-and-effect relationships. For example, in geography, understanding climate (dependent variable) means being able to describe the influence of factors like latitude, altitude, and currents (independent variables). In art history, artists' techniques and visual relationships (independent variables) create effects on viewers (dependent variable). In the study of law, precedents, evidence, and laws affect court decisions on particular cases. Similarly, in reasoning about moral situations, factors such as the consequences of behavior and the rights of affected parties influence moral judgments (Collins and Stevens 1982).

Inquiry methods are useful in teaching causal relationships and correcting misconceptions. An excellent analysis of inquiry methods is provided by Collins and Stevens (1982), who analyzed inquiry teachers' dialogues with students to identify goals and strategies they use to foster students' reasoning. Goals included teaching basic facts and concepts relevant to the topic, a specific rule or theory in a domain, and how to derive a rule or theory.

Teachers who use inquiry methods encourage students to analyze a situation in search of causal factors. They deliberately ask questions, select examples, and use "entrapment" strategies to elicit misconceptions in students' thinking so that they can be corrected.

The classroom agenda of inquiry teachers is characterized by high-level goals that enable them to respond flexibly to students' changing understanding. As goals are met, the teacher removes them from the agenda, often verbally checking them off with "clue words such as 'okay,' 'now,' or 'anyway' " (p. 89). Inquiry teachers also have priorities for modifying the agenda in response to the dialogue. For instance, they take care of errors in the theory before dealing with omitted factors, because errors can interfere with learning of other information. They introduce factors in causal or temporal sequences. And they call on students who have not participated before those who have so that all students have the opportunity to verbalize their thinking. Further, inquiry teachers have strategies for selecting cases that are most likely to achieve their goals. They choose more salient, frequent, or familiar cases (e.g., large countries in geography, major diseases in medicine, everyday problems in moral reasoning) over less common or less important ones. They also choose cases that lead to a "significant generalization" (p. 91).

The decisions inquiry teachers make in all these areas are influenced by their model of the students' understanding. The model includes estimates of what the students probably already know and knowledge of misconceptions that frequently occur in the subject domain (Collins and Stevens 1982).

Inquiry teaching has the advantage of providing students with models of problem solving. It also fosters motivation and increases understanding and applicability of the subject. On the other hand, information is communicated slowly; the method is most effective when students have read extensively on the topic before the dialogue. Further, teachers must be able to involve all students so that their ideas can be made explicit and corrected if necessary. The teacher must be very knowledgeable, flexible, and ingenious, especially in choosing problems for analysis (Collins and Stevens 1982).

While most professors value conceptual understanding, many underestimate the limitations of current methods of instruction as means to achieve it. Teaching for understanding requires *time*, a deep understanding of the subject on the part of the instructor, and perceptiveness in diagnosing students' problems in understanding.

Organization. The schemas developed by students are influenced by the organizational structure of the materials used to teach them (Eylon and Reif 1984). Unfortunately, teachers and textbooks often fail to point out the organizing principles, generalizations, or causal relationships that help students construct an adequate representation of the material (Armbruster 1984; Larkin 1979). Research in physics and history illustrates the advantages gained by emphasizing hierarchical structure in teaching.

Students' performance of complex tasks is enhanced when information is presented in hierarchical form, with information most relevant to the task placed at the top of the hierarchy (Eylon and Reif 1984). Three groups of students studied rules for solving physics problems. Students who received the information in a logical, linear, sequential fashion performed *less* effectively than students who were given a general procedure followed by the specific rules. Repeating the linear presentation improved the performance of high-ability students, who evidently used the second presentation to organize the material hierarchically; repetition did not help the poorer students.

In a second study, the researchers demonstrated that performance improves when the hierarchy is adapted to the demands of the task. Two hierarchies were constructed. In the deductive version, theoretical concepts were presented first, elaborated in the second level, and their historical development described in the third level. The hierarchy was reversed for the historical version. In each case, relationships between levels of the hierarchy were clearly explained in the text. When the task involved historical analysis, students who learned material organized historically performed best. When the task required students to generalize the model to a more complex situation, students who studied the deductive model performed best. In general, material at the top of the hierarchies was recalled best. The lowest-ability students in these studies appeared to be unable to reconstruct hierarchical structures in spite of the visual rehearsal strategies used to present it (Eylon and Reif 1984).

Freshmen in a study skills course who learned one of two methods for detecting hierarchical structure in historical texts were better able to learn from new material than those who learned nonhierarchical study methods (Slater et al. 1988). One group learned a visual model and used it over a nine-week period to generate summaries of text. A second group answered questions about main ideas and details in the text (also a hierarchical structure). Both groups discussed their responses with a partner during class and discussed or wrote out ideas recalled from the text. Control students received instruction in study skills, but the two structure groups outperformed the control group on all experimental measures.

In these studies, students learned best when they identified the underlying structure of the text and discussed their analysis with experimenters or peers.

Accessibility. People apparently need considerable prompting to use their knowledge to solve problems. For example, when reasoning about issues like litter laws, individuals offered more lines of argument as years of education increased (and therefore, presumably, the amount of information available for reasoning), but the increase was marginal (0.1 "lines" per year— Perkins 1985, 1986). When reasoning about arguments of personal significance, however, which they claimed to have thought about for hundreds of hours, people offered twice as many arguments. To demonstrate that more information was in fact available, interviewers asked content-free probing questions after initial arguments were offered by a group of 20 high schcol students. The probes significantly increased the number of arguments the students put forth (Perkins 1986).

Access to relevant knowledge is greatly reduced when the learner is *not* informed that the knowledge will be useful (Perfetto, Bransford, and Franks 1983). In an experiment, students rated the truthfulness of 12 statements directly relevant to several simple problems. After a three-minute delay, they were given the problems; for example:

> Uriah Fuller, the famous Israeli superpsychic, can tell you the score of any baseball game *before* the game starts. What is his secret?

One-third of the students were told explicitly that the information they had just rated was relevant, one-third were not prompted, and one-third did not receive the clue statements at all. Students who received the clues but no prompts to use them performed at the same level as those who had received *no* clues at all. Explicit prompting resulted in the best performance, although the mean proportion of responses using the cues was a surprisingly low .54. (Incidentally, the clue to the "psychic" problem is that at the beginning of any game, the score is 0 to 0.)

Providing a personally relevant context for new material may increase its accessibility. In a lecture, the concept of attention was presented to one group of students by relating it to situations students encounter daily (for example, studying or listening to a lecture). Another group simply learned about experiments on the subject. Both groups initially learned the material equally well. The "context" group, however, reported thinking about the concept more often in the following two days than those who simply learned about the experiments (Bransford et al. 1986).

Implications for instruction. Simply presenting declarative knowledge to students is no guarantee that they will be able to use it to solve problems, write essays, or think critically about issues for which the knowledge is relevant. It does not follow, however, that critical thinking tasks should be withheld from students until they have acquired a foundation of knowledge. Thinking about content helps students master new information. For example, when students write short essays about texts they have read, their conceptual understanding of the content is greater than when they either take notes or answer probing study questions. Most important, gains in understanding are greatest for students who began the task with low levels of passage-specific knowledge (Newell 1984). Writing analytical essays evokes more high-level reasoning processes than writing summaries (Durst 1987) or answering study questions (Newell 1984). Thinking tasks can build from short assignments focused on one or two key concepts to more complex assignments that encourage students to integrate ideas from many sources so that they simultaneously acquire knowledge and develop skill in using it.

Assign tasks that require the students to construct their own schemas, perhaps with the assistance of a peer.

Taking students' background knowledge in a subject into account is useful when planning critical thinking assignments. Assignments that assume intimate familiarity with the discipline beyond the level of the course may challenge a few students to unanticipated heights, but for many, the only recourse will be the sort of quote-and-paste hodgepodge that frustrates teachers and fosters students' negative views of academic inquiry. On the other hand, assignments that help students organize and develop the knowledge they are acquiring are likely to increase the quality of thinking they can do about the subject.

A pretest can help students determine whether they are adequately prepared for a particular course. Students whose preparation is marginal should be encouraged to review materials recommended by the professor or to consider taking a less advanced course on the subject.

In addition to these measures, helping students organize their knowledge of the subject increases their learning. In lectures, presenting material in a chart, matrix, or hierarchical outline helps students build an organizing schema that will assist them later in recalling the information, but it is probably equally important to assign tasks that require the students to construct their own schemas, perhaps with the assistance of a peer. Using familiar examples and analogies helps students relate content to existing schemas, especially important in the early stages of learning.

Some declarative knowledge about arguments may enhance critical thinking, for example, the forms and pitfalls discussed in the previous section. The role of such knowledge has not been explored in the cognitive literature. Students understand the basic "script" for presenting arguments; what they do not understand is the degree to which an argument must be developed to be convincing.

Procedural knowledge

Educators typically want students to use their knowledge to accomplish discipline-related tasks like solving problems, interpreting texts, designing or evaluating experiments, or weighing the merits of a proposal. Declarative knowledge suffices to talk or read about a subject; procedural knowledge makes it possible to *do* something in the subject domain (Greeno 1980; Larkin, Heller, and Greeno 1980; Simon 1980).

Procedural knowledge relevant to critical thinking includes knowledge of how information is obtained, analyzed, and communicated in a discipline (Loacker et al. 1984). For example, in art history, the task is to interpret works of art and describe their historical significance. Students must supplement declarative knowledge of art history with procedural knowledge necessary to decode the images in the painting, integrate visual and historical evidence, and present the interpretation in verbal form (Schmidt, McLaughlin, and Leighten n.d.). In economics, a typical task is to analyze the effects of changes in one segment of the economy on other segments (Voss et al. 1986). Other examples of domain-specific procedural knowledge include historical analysis in political science, setting up proofs in mathematics, and decomposing software problems to write computer programs (Voss, Tyler, and Yengo 1983). Students must learn a different "code" of procedural knowledge in each of several disciplines and eventually develop a moderate level of expertise in at least one area of specialized study.

Some aspects of the code are explicit and formalized, for example, the "scientific method." Others, however, are implicit, tacit, taken-for-granted thought processes that an expert uses without conscious attention. For example, the use of constraints by political science experts sets their solution procedures apart as qualitatively different from those of novice and intermediate students. Yet it is unlikely that this aspect of political science problem solving would be explicitly addressed in teaching, unless the instructional context included many examples of political science problem solving. Such a context would include modeling the process by the professor and multiple attempts to solve problems by the students. Even so, the professor would probably have to explicitly point out the use (or neglect) of constraints so that students would begin to take into account contextual factors in constructing plausible solutions.

Within the domain of social science problem solving, at least, teaching students to identify constraints before they propose solutions might help them to overcome a major weakness in their arguments: inadequate development. In comparison to experts' arguments, students' arguments are thin; for example, in the political science studies, experts averaged nearly nine levels of backing for their solutions, with long chains of supportive argument. Novices averaged fewer than three levels of backing and used very short chains of argument (Voss, Greene, Post, and Penner 1983). Similarly, in another case, students offered only a few lines of argument to support (and far fewer in opposition to) their views on current issues (Perkins 1985).

Constraints serve as criteria in the search for an adequate solution. Considering proposed solutions in light of constraints causes expert problem solvers to notice subproblems and implications of their suggestions, which in turn prompts them to modify or elaborate upon their solutions (Voss, Tyler, and Yengo 1983). *Without constraints, novices have no basis for evaluating proposed solutions or reasons in support of a claim and hence no stimulus for further inquiry.*

Procedural knowledge can be taught directly to students using a variety of methods that incorporate practice and feedback on the desired skill. An example is learning to write a good definition, with a clearly stated criterion and illustrative and contrastive examples. Students acquire the greatest skill when they are given examples that might illustrate a concept (such as courage) and asked to develop definitional criteria. Students who analyze extended definitions and write short definitions (standard instructional practice in many composition classrooms) show no significant gains in the overall quality of their definitions or in the use of criteria and examples. Neither approach significantly influences students' ability to generate contrastive examples, however (Hillocks, Kahn, and Johannessen 1983). In composition instruction generally, writing improves most when students use inquiry strategies to develop their essays (Hillocks 1984, 1986).

In physics, explicit instruction on strategies used by experts improves beginners' ability to solve problems. Expert physicists integrate principles when solving problems, but instruction in physics typically teaches principles individually in succession, without showing students how to integrate them to solve problems and with a premature emphasis on mathematical representation. Larkin and Reif (1979) taught students in introductory physics how to use several physics principles in concert to solve problems as well as how to approach problems by constructing "low-detail qualitative descriptions" (p. 199), then successively refining their strategy. A control group studied the same principles, but instruction reinforced attention to mathematical descriptions. Although both groups learned the individual principles equally well, all five students in the qualitative group solved two or three problems within the given time limit, but four of the five in the mathematical group solved only one problem (the fifth solved three). The authors concluded that students should be encouraged to use "vague verbal or pictorial descriptions" in the early stages of problem solving (as expert physicists do), then taught how to translate them into precise mathematical form during the problem-solving process (p. 201).

Perhaps practice enables declarative knowledge about the procedure to become procedural knowledge mediated by verbal self-instructions, which gradually fade as the procedure becomes more automated (Anderson 1985). This model helps to understand why experts often have difficulty verbalizing their procedural knowledge—and may not even be aware they are using it. They can perform a task (such as construct geometric proofs), but they cannot describe or analyze their own actions; moreover, they attribute students' performance on reasoning tasks to "intelligence" or "motivation" (Greeno 1980).

Students probably induce strategic knowledge from working problems and watching teachers solve them (Greeno 1980). The strategies experts use to solve problems may become public only when an unexpectedly difficult question causes the teacher to "think out loud," giving students a momentary glimpse of the workings of an expert's mind. Unfortunately, such moments are rare, particularly in subjects where time is considered precious and teachers conscientiously come "prepared," as in the case of math professors who believe they must cover several problems to make the session worthwhile and so have worked out the problems for the day to avoid "wasting time" on incorrect solutions. In contrast, thinking aloud while solving a problem, perhaps inviting the class to participate in exploring it, gives students a vivid image of experts' actual thought processes.

Metacognition and implications for instruction

A third factor influencing problem solving is metacognition, the use of strategies to monitor and control attention and memory and to make decisions about how to proceed on a task (Collins, Brown, and Newman 1986; Flavell 1976, 1979; Palincsar and

Brown 1984; Schoenfeld 1983a, 1983b, 1985a, 1985b; Weinstein and Rogers 1985). Metacognition is distinct from procedural knowledge in that procedural knowledge is domain specific, while metacognitive strategies support problem solving in any domain.

Planning is an important metacognitive strategy, visible in expert reasoning in many domains. Experts plan by establishing goals and subgoals during the problem-solving process. Experts also use a variety of strategies to review their progress. For example, in writing they monitor the correspondence between the text and their intent (Flower and Hayes 1980; Flower et al. 1986). Effective readers monitor their comprehension using strategies like summarizing key points, questioning the meaning and implications of the text, clarifying the text by rereading when a "triggering event" (such as inability to summarize a passage adequately) signals a failure in comprehension, and predicting what might lie ahead in the text (Palincsar and Brown 1984). Mathematicians and physicists, too, remain alert to clues that a solution may not be working and revise their approach accordingly.

Students can learn to use metacognitive strategies to increase the effectiveness of their reading and problem solving. For example, in a training program focused on metacognition in mathematical problem solving, students learned to consider several possible solution strategies, to evaluate each one, and to check their progress after five minutes of implementation. Students who completed the 18-day course engaged in significantly more planning before attempting a solution to a problem and reviewed their progress far more frequently than before the course (Schoenfeld 1985a). Moreover, the program enhanced students' use of knowledge about mathematical problems. After the course, they categorized mathematics problems in ways that more closely corresponded to the categories used by mathematicians. A control group that learned a "structured, hierarchical, and orderly way to solve nonmathematical problems using the computer" showed no similar improvement (Schoenfeld and Herrmann 1982, p. 486). This result suggests that training in metacognition makes knowledge more accessible to students.

Some experimental metacognitive strategies can be adapted for classroom use. One study, for example, paired students and assigned them text passages to study and summarize in writing (Spurlin et al. 1984). Students who took turns actively questioning each other outperformed students who were less active or who worked alone. The active pairs used metacognitive questions to monitor accuracy and to encourage each other to relate the text to prior knowledge. Similar questions can be given to students (or developed in class discussion) and used in studying or in small groups.

Work in small groups can also incorporate a strategy called "pair problem solving." One student solves a problem out loud while the other acts as a monitor, asking questions whenever something seems unclear or incomplete. A checklist helps the listener detect errors and omissions in the problem solver's reasoning (Lochhead and Whimbey 1987; Whimbey and Lochhead 1982). This approach, combined with training on formal reasoning abilities using the Piagetian learning cycle model, is credited with the academic success of minority students who have completed Xavier University's SOAR program (Lochhead and Whimbey 1987; Whimbey et al. 1980).

Finally, teachers can follow Schoenfeld's lead in mathematics, demonstrating their own metacognitive processes, just as they can demonstrate procedural knowledge at work. Many study skills programs include training in metacognition. These programs teach students to become aware of their own cognitions, to establish learning goals, to assess progress toward their goals, and to modify their learning strategies when necessary (see, for example, Weinstein and Rogers 1985). Training in comprehension monitoring has proven useful in bolstering students' reading performance (Palincsar and Brown 1984; Weinstein and Rogers 1985). Teaching students to formulate questions during lecture and reading significantly affects their grade point average and persistence in college (Heiman and Slomianko 1984). In their classes, the professor can demonstrate a careful reading of a difficult text passage, showing students the techniques of questioning, summarizing, clarifying, and predicting, as well as relating the information to previously studied material and encouraging students to use these techniques on assignments.

Metacognitive processes help to manage large quantities of complex and often conflicting information (including lengthy arguments composed by experts) encountered in critical thinking. School practices, such as lecturing from textbooks and using only "objective" examinations, discourage the development of metacognitive skills other than, perhaps, the use of mnemonic devices. In contrast, instruction that directs students' attention to their own reasoning processes or that creates a way for students to stimulate each others' metacognitions aids learning and may improve performance on related cognitive tasks (see, for example, Palincsar and Brown 1984; Weinstein and Rogers 1985; Whimbey et al. 1980). Metacognitive skills have the potential to increase students' ability to learn and to use what they know (Scardamalia and Bereiter 1986).

Metacognition may play an important role in developing objectivity, because it enables people to search out relevant knowledge and to reflect on their reasoning. In a study described earlier, metacognitive questions posed to 20 high school students after they had offered their arguments on an issue significantly increased the number of arguments they provided on both their own and the opposing side (Perkins 1986). "My-side" arguments doubled to more than seven, while "other-side" arguments increased by 700 percent, to 5.6. In other words, simply by prompting, the researcher was able to enrich the array of reasons students used to develop their positions.

The study offers less reason for optimism than might appear at first glance, however. Despite the dramatic change in both the number and proportion of arguments offered on the opposing side, only three students changed their minds on the issue. For the remaining 17, the new information they retrieved had almost no effect on the confidence with which they held their initial position. The study demonstrates the resilience of beliefs in the face of contrary evidence, confirming results reported by others (Dressel and Lehmann 1965; Lord, Ross, and Leper 1979; Ross and Anderson 1982). Students actively resist requests to present arguments for an opposing view (Alvermann, Dillon, and O'Brien 1987; Bernstein 1988; Roby 1983, 1985). They also evaluate studies that favor their point of view more positively than those that do not, a phenomenon labeled "biased assimilation" (Lord, Ross, and Leper 1979). Persuading students to weigh information objectively poses a far more perplexing challenge to teachers than does teaching them how to retrieve it.

To counteract biased assimilation of evidence, use of the heuristic has been suggested (Bernstein 1988), what some have called "consider the opposite" (Lord, Ross, and Leper 1979). When reviewing research, students are instructed to ask themselves whether they would have produced the same evaluation of the research if it had produced the opposite result. The "devil's advocate" is used to encourage students to take the point of view of others, essentially a request to state the point of view of someone the student disagrees with to that person's satisfaction (Roby 1983, 1985).

Professors who want to facilitate their students' ability to reason about disciplinary content can use their awareness of metacognition to help students become more strategic learners. They can demonstrate and discuss their approaches to solving tough problems or reading difficult material. In this way, content can be clarified while metacognitive skills are introduced. Professors can also conduct class discussions in which students share their approaches to assignments that require critical thinking and collaborate to devise techniques for addressing problems they identify while the work is in progress. Guidelines for group work, class discussion, or assignments may also include metacognitive questions or prompts like those described here.

Beliefs about Knowledge

Beliefs about the nature of knowledge in the discipline under study influence the approaches individuals adopt when solving complex thinking tasks in that discipline (Ryan 1984a, 1984b; Schoenfeld 1983a, 1985b). An example is the belief that history consists of a chronology of known events and that the main task is to learn important dates. This belief directs students' attention inappropriately in lecture and reading, making it difficult for them to perceive important information, such as multiple causes or alternative interpretations of events.

With respect to informal argument, students do not share academics' belief that extended analysis of an issue is necessary. They are satisfied to offer a few arguments for one or another point of view and accept it because it fits their existing beliefs—what one writer refers to as a "make-sense epistemology" (Perkins 1986; Perkins, Allen, and Hafner 1983) and another as "epistemic cognition" (Kitchener 1983). Developmental studies, discussed in the next section, have documented widespread adherence to this view of thinking among college students (e.g., Kitchener and King 1981; Welfel 1982).

Epistemological beliefs can have a devastating impact on students' problem solving. For example, many students in mathematics appear to hold a "nonmathematical epistemology," which includes beliefs such as "Mathematics problems are always solved in less than 10 minutes, if they are solved at all. Corollary: Give up after 10 minutes." and "Only geniuses are capable of discovering or creating mathematics. First corollary: If you forget something, too bad. After all, you're not a genius and you won't be able to derive it on your own. Second corollary: Accept procedures at face value, and don't try to understand why they work" (Schoenfeld 1985b, p. 372). A parallel exists between students' failure to recognize mathematical argumentation as useful and the "make-sense epistemology" mentioned earlier (Schoenfeld 1983a, 1983b, 1985a, 1985b).

Cognitive psychologists, with the exception of Schoenfeld, have paid little attention to the ways in which belief systems change or the nature of their influence on learning and reasoning. Schoenfeld (1985a) illustrates changes in students' beliefs about mathematics as a consequence of participation in his problem-solving course. Students exchanged their initial reliance on trial-and-error exploration for analysis and deduction, they paid more attention to the meaning than the form of problems, and they became active rather than passive in solving problems. (Although these changes reflect adoption of new procedural and metacognitive strategies, Schoenfeld infers from them a change in students' beliefs about the meaning of their task.)

Affective Factors: Curiosity and Purpose
Although the role of affective factors in critical thinking deserves greater attention, few cognitive researchers have explored it empirically. Three cognitive factors that arouse intrinsic motivation have been identified (Malone 1981), however, and two studies suggest the role of peers in fostering motivation for learning.

Intrinsic motivation arises when the student perceives a situation as problematic. The key factors in intrinsic motivation are *curiosity, challenge,* and *fantasy.* Curiosity is aroused when learners experience inadequacies in their knowledge (e.g., upon completing the penultimate chapter of a murder mystery). Malone notes that inadequacies can be exposed using the inquiry or "Socratic" instructional methods summarized above (see Collins and Stevens 1982). Challenge requires personally meaningful goals, uncertain outcomes, and difficulty levels and feedback that enhance rather than damage self-esteem. Fantasy intrinsic to the subject (as in a game that presents realistic problems and naturalistic feedback) enhances both learning and intrinsic motivation. Informative feedback also facilitates intrinsic motivation (Malone 1981).

Students' orientation to peers can also be used to give purpose to learning. In one study, students were given a passage to study. One group was told that they would be tested on the material; the other group was told that they would teach the material to another student, who would then be tested. In fact, both groups were tested. Students in the peer-teaching group spent more time on the material, rated themselves as more active in the learning process, and performed better on both informational and conceptual tests than students who were simply studying for themselves (Benware and Deci 1984). In another study, conducted with middle-school children, students who worked in cooperatively structured groups to analyze controversial issues engaged in more voluntary search for additional materials relevant to the topic than students working alone or in competitively structured groups. Interestingly, they also incorporated more arguments from the opposing viewpoint into their final individual papers than did students in the other two groups (Johnson and Johnson 1985).

These studies suggest that students' motivation can be influenced through both the structure of the presentation of material and the social structure of the classroom.

Conclusions

The research reviewed here has several broad implications for faculty who wish to foster students' abilities in critical thinking.

1. Arouse students' curiosity by using problems as organizing principles for instruction. Link new information to the context in which it is to be used and to students' background knowledge and intuitive conceptions of the subject. Use task-adapted hierarchies, inquiry methods, and familiar examples to enhance understanding, organization, and accessibility of declarative knowledge.
2. Teach students when and how to use what they are learning. Use modeling, coaching, practice, and feedback to teach reasoning skills relevant to the subject of study.
3. Demonstrate metacognition and build metacognitive prompts into class exercises and assignments.
4. Elicit and discuss beliefs about the nature of what is to be learned and provide experiences to overcome students' naive conceptions about the subject.
5. Use social and cognitive strategies to enhance purpose and motivation to learn.

These conclusions suggest a "cognitive apprenticeship" approach to instruction (Collins, Brown, and Newman 1986). The elements of a cognitive apprenticeship are modeling (demonstrating a cognitive task so students can observe it), coaching (assisting the learner during learning or performance of a task), scaffolding (providing expert guidance initially and gradually removing it), articulating (reasoning processes and knowledge in use), reflecting (comparing students' problem-solving processes with those of an expert), and exploring (encouraging students to establish their own goals or subgoals within a given task). Instruction in an apprenticeship is sequenced for increasing complexity and diversity and progresses from global to local skills. The sociological aspects of the apprenticeship include "situated learning" (learning in the context of a task or problem similar to the context of actual use), a "culture of expert practice" (in which students enact and communicate about the skills they are to learn), intrinsic motivation, and use of both cooperative and competitive activity structures (Collins, Brown, and Newman 1986).

Integrating multiple forms of knowledge in instruction offers a coherent way to ensure that students will take from their education a rich and accessible store of knowledge and skills. The time required to point out to students the structural features of arguments and the characteristics of domain-specific reasoning is small compared to the potential benefits of having a framework and a common language for discussing academic work.

In spite of professors' best efforts to foster critical thinking, difficulties will arise. Students may acquire the form but not the substance of critical thinking (Nickerson 1986b; Stern and Cope 1956; Walters 1986). While some of these difficulties arise from students' limited background knowledge, others reflect their intuitive conceptions about the nature of knowledge and the learning process. The next section describes the evolution of students' beliefs about knowledge and considers the ways these beliefs interact with instruction intended to foster critical thinking.

DEVELOPMENTAL FOUNDATIONS OF CRITICAL THINKING

If critical thinking were only a matter of acquiring skills and knowledge, teaching students to do it would be relatively unproblematic. Evidence already cited, however, suggests that this is not the case. Students' difficulties with critical thinking can be better understood by considering the assumptions about knowledge, truth, authority, and inquiry implicit in the process itself.

Critical thinking takes pluralism as given and sees individuals as responsible for constructing their own coherent account of whatever subject they are disposed to investigate. This relativistic or constructivist theory about what it means to know something is not necessarily held by people in students' home communities (Belenky et al. 1985, 1986; Bizell 1986; Daly 1986). Discrepancies between students' and professors' assumptions about knowledge probably account for a major share of the frustration both groups experience when critical thinking is required in a course. Models of college students' intellectual development provide a framework for understanding how students come to terms with this discrepancy and what teachers can do to help.

Constructed knowledge as described in **Women's Ways of Knowing** *captures the interplay of rationality, caring, and commitment that is the ultimate goal of education.*

Background of the Research

The first studies of epistemological development in college were conducted at Harvard by William Perry and his associates (Perry 1970). They interviewed over 100 students, nearly all male, in two separate four-year studies at Harvard and Radcliffe in the late 1950s and early 1960s. Eighty-four of these students were interviewed during each of their four years in college. The first set of interviews was used to generate the scheme; the second set provided a test of the scheme's validity.

Since then, researchers have modified Perry's formulation of intellectual development (Kitchener and King 1981) or tested its underlying assumptions (Clinchy and Zimmerman 1982; Kurfiss 1975, 1977). Many others have explored its implications for learning and educational practice (e.g., Baxter-Magolda 1987; Clinchy, Lief, and Young 1977; Goldberger 1981; King 1985; Knefelkamp 1974; Knefelkamp and Slepitza 1976; Ryan 1984a, 1984b; Schmidt and Davison 1983; Stephenson and Hunt 1977; Touchton et al. 1977; Widick and Simpson 1978). Measures for assessing epistemological development have been developed and validated, using interviews (Kitchener and King 1981) or paper-and-pencil assessments (Baxter-Magolda and Porterfield 1985; Knefelkamp and Moore n.d.;

Mentkowski, Moeser, and Strait 1983). Finally, several studies have examined connections between epistemological models and other aspects of development and experience (e.g., Benack 1984; Benack and Basseches 1987; Brabeck 1983; King, Kitchener, and Wood 1985; Kurfiss 1975, 1976, 1977; Welfel 1982). (For reviews of research on the Perry model, see King 1978 and Perry 1981.)[1]

Research on women's epistemological development has shown that while the broad categories of the scheme are similar to those identified by Perry, contemporary women frequently differ from the men and women interviewed by Perry in their views of authority, truth, and knowledge (Belenky et al. 1986; Benack 1982).

"Stages" of Intellectual Development[2]

Perry (1970) identified nine sequential "positions from which a person views his world" (p. 48) and three "alternatives to growth" (p. 177ff). Belenky and associates identified four perspectives among college women and an additional perspective among women who were clients in human service agencies. The following summary of intellectual development in college integrates Belenky and associates' extensive research on women's perspectives with the earlier findings reported by Perry. The summary is organized into four major categories or levels and suggests how students at each developmental level will respond to tasks that require critical thinking.

Level 1: Dualism/received knowledge

Many students believe that knowledge is a collection of discrete facts; therefore, learning is simply a matter of acquiring information delivered by the professor in concert with the text. Information is either correct or it is not; hence, Perry's label for this belief system is "dualism." Dualistic thinkers do not realize the degree to which the information presented in a course or textbook is selected, interpreted, and systematized. They view the professor as the authority, presenting factual knowledge

---

1. William S. Moore coordinates the Perry Network; his address is 1670 Prince Ave., Athens, GA 30606.
2. The term "stages" implies a more deterministic and integrative concept of development than researchers in this field wish to claim. For this reason, Perry chose the more modest term "positions," and Belenky and associates chose "perspectives."

known to all experts in the discipline. Their dependence on authority as the source of all knowledge led Belenky and her associates to refer to this belief system as "received knowledge." Professors are always more or less right in this view, because, as one student says, "They have books to look at. Things that you look up in a book, you normally get the right answer" (Belenky et al. 1986, p. 39).

For these students, the concept of interpretation, essential to critical thinking, is puzzling. Doesn't the text mean what it says? Why can't the author just say what he or she means? They may become confused or indignant when professors ask them to reason independently. Here is one student's response to a general education course that emphasizes thinking:

> "It's supposed to teach you to—ah, reason better. That seems to be the, the excuse that natural science people give for these courses—they're supposed to teach you to arrive at more logical conclusions and look at things in a more scientific manner. Actually, what you get out of that course is you, you get an idea that science is a terrifically confused thing in which nobody knows what's coming off anyway" (Perry 1970, p. 74).

In the face of "so many conflicting doctrines and opinions," many students in this first level opt "just to keep quiet until [they] really know just what the answer is" (Perry 1970, p. 87). Rather than reflecting a personality characteristic like "passivity" or "vocationalism," their resistance to critical thinking reflects a legitimate developmental quandary as they encounter a world far more complex than they have realized.

Level 2: Multiplicity/subjective knowledge

Before students can accept the challenges and responsibilities of independent thinking, they must recognize that "conflicting doctrines and opinions" are an inevitable and legitimate feature of knowledge. And they must begin to develop trust in their "inner voices" as a source of knowledge. This is the work of the second level of intellectual development as described by Perry and by Belenky and associates.

In some courses, particularly those in the humanities and social sciences, students encounter numerous conflicts of interpretation and theory. Most students gradually acknowledge the existence of unknowns, doubts, and uncertainties, at least in *some* areas of knowledge. When the facts are not known, knowledge is a matter of "mere opinion." When no absolute truth exists, one "opinion" is as good as another, and teachers "have no right to call [the student] wrong" on matters of opinion (Perry 1970, p. 97). Many conflicts over grades probably arise from students' failure to understand, or professors' failure to communicate, the criteria used to judge "opinion" papers.

Perry's term "multiplicity" emphasizes this position's departure from dichotomous thinking. Belenky and associates' term "subjective knowledge" highlights women's tendency to turn inward, away from external authorities as their primary source of knowledge. The majority of college students subscribe to this category of epistemological beliefs (Belenky et al. 1986; King, Kitchener, and Wood 1985; Welfel 1982).

Multiplicity/subjective knowledge is a crucial turning point in the development of critical thinking. Students at this level recognize complexity but have not yet learned how to navigate its waters. They perceive no basis other than intuition, feeling, or "common sense" on which to judge the merits of the opinions they now accept as reflections of legitimate differences. They are "make-sense epistemologists" (Perkins, Allen, and Hafner 1983) in their studies of informal argument. A recent popular characterization describes these students as suffering from the "openness of indifference" (Bloom 1987, p. 41). "Openness used to be the virtue that permitted us to seek the good by using reason. It now means accepting everything and denying reason's power" (p. 38).

Level 3: Relativism/procedural knowledge

Insistent pressure from peers (for example, in arguments in the residence hall or coffee shop) and from faculty (to give reasons for opinions offered in class discussions, on examinations, or in term papers) leads some students to realize that "opinions" differ in quality. Good opinions are supported with *reasons*. Students learn that they must examine an issue "in complex terms, weighing more than one factor in trying to develop your own opinion" (Perry 1970, p. 100). In the arts, students learn that they must substitute analysis using "objective" criteria based on factors in the work for personal responses to its mood and character (Belenky et al. 1986). Belenky and associates' term "procedural knowledge" captures this emphasis on using disciplinary methods of reasoning. Perry labels this belief system "relativism," because it assumes that what counts as true depends on (is relative to) the frame of reference used to evaluate the phenomenon in question. Confusion about the meaning of the term "relativism" has led many writers to use the term "contextualism" or "contextual relativism" (see, for example, Clinchy and Zimmerman 1982). Others have used the terms "reflective skepticism" (McPeck 1981) and "critical epistemology" (Perkins, Allen, and Hafner 1983) to describe this way of thinking.

Level 3 beliefs reflect the traditional academic view of reasoning as objective analysis and argument. Belenky and associates noticed, however, that some women employed an alternative procedure for developing opinions, which they called "connected knowledge." Connected knowledge attempts to understand the reasons for another's way of thinking. The student undertakes a "deliberate, imaginative extension of one's understanding into positions that initially feel wrong or remote" (p. 121). Connected knowledge differs from the objective analytical model of thinking, which they called "separate knowledge." Confronting a poem, separate knowers ask, "What techniques can I use to analyze it?" In contrast, connected knowers ask, "What is this poet trying to say to me?" (Belenky et al. 1986, p. 101). Connected knowledge does not preclude analysis or criticism; it does, however, begin with a more empathic treatment of divergent views.

In Perry's study, most students came to realize that the "academic" method of deciding issues is generally applicable, because knowledge is inherently indeterminate. Subsequent studies have found fewer than half of college seniors subscribing to this epistemological perspective (Baxter-Magolda and Porterfield 1985; King, Kitchener, and Wood 1985; Welfel 1982).

Level 4: Commitment in relativism/constructed knowledge
The reasoning procedures of level 3 illuminate a situation, but they do not provide definitive answers. Ultimately, individuals must take a position and make commitments, even though they can have no external assurances of the "correctness" of what they choose to do or believe. Hence, Perry labels this perspective "commitment in relativism."

"Constructed knowledge," as described by Belenky and associates, integrates knowledge learned from others with the "inner truth" of experience and personal reflection. At this level, students understand that knower and known are intimately intertwined and exist in a particular historical and cultural context. Even in the sciences, this realization is possible, as one senior honors student observes:

> "In science you don't really want to say that something's true. You realize that you're dealing with a model. Our models are always simpler than the real world. The real world is more complex than anything we can create. We're simplifying everything so that we can work with it, but the thing is really more complex. When you try to describe things, you're leaving the truth because you're oversimplifying" (Belenky et al. 1986, p. 138).

Constructed knowledge as described in *Women's Ways of Knowing* captures the interplay of rationality, caring, and commitment that is the ultimate goal of education. Constructed knowers are able to take "a position outside a particular context or frame of reference and look back on 'who' is asking the question, 'why' the question is asked at all, and 'how' answers are arrived at" (Belenky et al. 1986, p. 139). They include the *self* in their knowing process, no longer executing a procedure but now becoming passionately engaged in the search for understanding. They are committed to nurturing rather than criticizing ideas; they may withdraw into silence if they believe the other person is not really listening, be it spouse, acquaintance, professor, or colleague. They seek integrated, authentic lives that contribute to "empowerment and improvement in the quality of life of others" (p. 152).

Alternatives to growth

Perry identified three alternatives to intellectual growth in the students he interviewed. *Temporizing* is "a pause in growth over a full academic year" (p. 178), *retreat* is a regression to an earlier position, and *escape* may take the form of fatalistic acceptance or gamesmanship. The common theme of these alternatives is, for Perry, the "defeat of care . . . . The speaker always conveys a nostalgia for a care and involvement that once was, or might have been, or might yet be . . . if only . . . " (p. 200).

Differences between Samples

Although the general outlines of these two developmental models are similar, Belenky and associates found several differences between the women in their sample and the men and women in Perry's study.

Most noticeably, particularly in level 1, the men at Harvard identified with the male authority figures they were discussing. In contrast, women in the sample tended not to identify with authorities. The absence of women in key positions in their schools and the negative attitudes toward women's capabilities conveyed by some professors provided little basis for identification, even among women from elite schools in the study.

A second difference is that for women, a central theme is their responsibility to help others. Although it may have been an issue for students at Harvard and Radcliffe, Perry did not explicitly identify it.

A third difference is that for the women interviewed by Belenky and associates, listening or gaining a voice is the dominant metaphor, with a new meaning at each level. Women in the perspective of received knowledge (level 1) report being strongly influenced—and confused—by advice from friends and counselors or by different views in what they read. Expecting to find "answers" outside themselves, they are unable to listen to their own voices, whether to express themselves in class or to decide what to do with their lives. They "resolve" this difficulty by valuing their inner voices almost exclusively in level 2, subjective knowledge. In level 3, procedural knowledge, the outer voice again becomes salient, now telling students *how* to think rather than *what* to think. Level 4, constructed knowledge, describes the integration of inner and outer voices. The metaphor of listening favors interaction with others as a way of knowing. In contrast, Perry's interviewees developed objectivity and distance as ways of knowing, implying an underlying metaphor of *seeing* (Belenky et al. 1986).

Yet another difference is the discovery by Belenky and associates of a perspective that *precedes* dualism/received knowledge. They call this perspective "silence." It is a powerless, dependent view of the self in which the women feared the power of words and cowered in the face of male authority. These women accepted sex-role stereotypes unquestioningly and accepted violence and brutality from men rather than live without them. Escape from silence often occurred when, as new mothers, they visited children's health centers where knowledgeable, supportive professionals treated them with respect and helped them develop confidence in their ability to learn. Silence was not found among women in the college sample, but the researchers found that many female students had a history of abuse by male authority figures, perhaps accounting for their reluctance to speak and their failure to identify readily with academic authority figures who are so often male (Belenky et al. 1986). Silent knowers share characteristics of illiterate peasants (Freire 1985). Like the women who discovered their own powers of learning, these peasants were "liberated" when they discovered that words could be used to shape the environment they had once thought of as immutable.

A final difference is the discovery of "connected knowledge" as a procedure used to understand unfamiliar ideas. Connected knowledge enables students to develop the supportive relationships that facilitate honest criticism. When teaching students who do not trust or identify with authorities, professors may find an emphasis on connected knowledge breaks down barriers to participation.

Criticisms

Perry's model, although widely used and appreciated by faculty in many disciplines, is not without its critics. For example, Perry himself notes that the beliefs clustered here as "level 4" cease to be epistemological, reflecting instead issues of personal identity, or in Perry's words, "emotional and aesthetic assessments" (p. 205). A proposed alternative, reflective judgment, is a seven-stage model that is more rigorously epistemological (Kitchener and King 1981). The reflective judgment interview asks students to reason about four epistemological dilemmas, such as how one would decide whether a particular food additive is safe. Responses are categorized on three "dimensions" (e.g., cognitive complexity, openness) and seven "content areas" (e.g., view of the nature of knowledge, role of authority, use of evidence) (King 1977, pp. 217–57; see also Kitchener 1977).

The reflective judgment interview has been extensively validated and has provided longitudinal data suggesting a clear directional trend in epistemological development and a significant influence of educational experiences (King et al. 1983; King, Kitchener, and Wood 1985).

Perry's scheme is often taken to mean that students' development is unified, coherent, and linear. Perry himself made no such claim. His choice of the term "positions" reflects his desire to avoid the implications of coherence and endurance implicit in the developmental construct of a "stage." He reports a study in which students' "positions" were rated in five "content-sectors"(academic, extracurricular, interpersonal, vocational, and religious) as well as in overall development or central tendency. The "ratings revealed a considerable disparity in the student's development from sector to sector . . . " (p. 48). Similarly, in another study, students' comprehension of short passages sequenced according to Perry's model was not consistent across a set of five topics related to academic learning and personal decision making (Kurfiss 1977). Another researcher found that women's responses on different topics failed to fall neatly into categories outlined by Perry (Benack 1982). Perhaps disparities in students' understanding of the same position when presented in different content areas reflects differences in their experience in each area (Kurfiss 1977).

Some criticisms of developmental theory are based on misconceptions about what the theories themselves claim. For example, Perry's model has been criticized as suggesting a rigidly linear, maturationist view of intellectual growth (Berthoff 1984), for being insensitive to cultural differences (Bizell 1984, 1986), and for confusing "development" with knowledge of the "conventions" of academic discourse, particularly argumentation (Kogen 1986). These criticisms and related misconceptions about developmental models in general have been analyzed in detail (Hays 1987).

Hays refutes the view that developmental models imply rigid tracking of students in the sense of restricting their intellectual diet to a "comfortable" level. According to Hays, an English professor and composition researcher, developmental theory provides useful insights about why some pedagogies (for example, the highly unstructured "natural process" method of teaching writing) are less effective with some students (for example, dualists/received knowers) because they fail to meet their developmental needs (in this case, the need for structure at least in the initial stages of learning). Developmental theory illuminates students' difficulties in learning to write arguments (Hays 1987; Hays, Brandt, and Chantry 1988); it also suggests how a curriculum might be sequenced to address students' needs more effectively. But categorizing students on the basis of fragmentary evidence is risky business and should be approached responsibly, with the aim of understanding and teaching students more effectively (Hays 1987).

Finally, the two developmental models described here have been criticized for their individualistic view of epistemology.

Perry's concept of contextual relativism does not address the socially constructed nature of the contexts themselves (Broughton 1975). Nor does it question the narrow "drive to advance the self" implied by Perry's highest positions (Harding 1987). "The study's sample includes no women who had the experience of acting collectively in order to change social conditions: Shouldn't this gap make us question the authors' claims about the 'highest' modes of knowledge seeking? Don't they miss something important here—the voices of women aware of the power of women thinking and working together to improve our lives?" (Harding 1987, p. 7). The gap is ironic, as the research was clearly a collaborative project (Harding 1987). The question implies that if cooperative learning becomes more commonplace in schools (as many educators predict or at least hope that it will), epistemological conceptions of future college students—and their professors—will be radically altered.

Relationship to Critical Thinking

Critical thinking skills (as measured by the Watson-Glaser Critical Thinking Appraisal) are probably *necessary* but not *sufficient* for progress to the higher levels of epistemological development. One researcher compared reflective judgment scores of students who scored either very high or very low on the Watson-Glaser assessment (Brabeck 1983). Four educational levels from high school to masters' program were represented; pairs were matched on educational level but differed in assessed critical thinking ability. The two measures were moderately correlated ($r = .40$). Low scorers on the critical thinking test generally scored no higher than stage 4 on the reflective judgment interview. In contrast, 30 percent of the high critical thinking group scored above stage 4 (late multiplicity in Perry's terms). Low-scoring critical thinkers scored no higher than stage 4; the high-scoring groups' maximum was stage 5 (early contextual relativism in Perry's scheme).

The findings support the hypothesis that students who have not learned the "basic skills" of critical thinking subscribe to epistemological views no higher than multiplicity. Students who have learned these skills may indeed progress into a stage equivalent to relativism but do not necessarily do so.

The study illustrates the limitations of instruction in the skills of analyzing and constructing arguments: *Learning these skills does not necessarily alter students' beliefs about the nature of truth or about their role in the construction of knowledge.* Epistemological beliefs change slowly (at most one stage in two years—King et al. 1983), and under present educational conditions, contextual relativism is uncommon even among college seniors (Belenky et al. 1986; King et al. 1983; King, Kitchener, and Wood 1985; Kitchener and King 1981; Welfel 1982). Researchers have found evidence, however, that higher levels of development can be achieved in developmentally supportive contexts (e.g., Clinchy, Lief, and Young 1977) and using developmental principles to plan disciplinary or interdisciplinary instruction (Knefelkamp 1974; Knefelkamp and Slepitza 1976; Widick, Knefelkamp, and Parker 1975; Widick and Simpson 1978).

Relationship to Other Behaviors

Some "novice" behaviors described in the section on cognitive psychology have been linked experimentally to students' progress on Perry's scheme. Relationships have been demonstrated between students' beliefs about knowledge and their reading habits, writing standards and performance, and performance in a survey course in psychology (Ryan 1984a, 1984b). Students who agreed with dualistic statements about learning reported reading textbooks for factual knowledge. Their preferred reading strategy was to "recall information from text in response to study guide questions" (Ryan 1984b, p. 252). In contrast, students who disagreed with the dualistic statements, and were thus inferred to subscribe to a more relativistic epistemology, read textbooks in search of conceptual relationships and meaning.

Further, students classified as relativists received higher course grades than those classified as dualists, with the effects of previous academic experience and SAT scores removed (Ryan 1984b). Perhaps, therefore, students' epistemological beliefs generate standards for monitoring text comprehension (Ryan 1984b). Higher standards yield greater comprehension, resulting in superior grades in survey courses where mastery of the text is a major element of performance.

Further, relativistic students used mature criteria for judging organization in written texts (Ryan 1984a). Relativists more often stated that a text must have an organizing principle, either a logical sequence of ideas or a unifying thesis. Dualists more often expressed criteria reflecting informativeness or a simple

Students who do not realize that knowledge is contextual may use critical thinking techniques to bolster their preconceived ideas of what is right.

grouping of information. And relativists produced more coherent prose when writing a short informative essay in response to a probe about their study behaviors.

A strong association was found to exist between students' epistemological assumptions and the rhetorical strategies they used to persuade a hostile audience of the value of their position on a controversial topic, implementation of tougher drunk driving laws (Hays, Brandt, and Chantry 1988). Rhetorical categories included dogmatic assertions, emotional appeals (including dramatic anecdotes), appeal to facts, logical analysis, and appeal to ethical principles or values. Dualistic students used dogmatic, moralistic assertions and some factual information but no logical analysis, as "presumably their assertions were grounded in a priori truth and needed no such justification" (p. 44). Multiplists offered factual information and problem-solving strategies but seldom used logical analysis. Students whose level of intellectual development included relativistic beliefs used logical analysis and some ethical appeals. They also used more effective audience strategies: building bridges of agreement with the audience, developing their arguments by anticipating possible objections, and offering abundant evidence to support their views. Their responses reflect awareness of context and realization that the assumptions one makes in presenting an argument are not necessarily shared by readers, especially opponents.

Developmental level was a more significant factor in the overall quality of students' writing than was the students' educational level (high school senior to college senior) (Hays, Brandt, and Chantry 1988). Thus, "genuine cognitive thresholds" make it difficult for some students to argue effectively. Sequenced writing instruction and attention to strategies for responding to oppositional readers are recommended to "force writers to explore perspectives and people different from themselves and so loosen their ontological rigidity. Such processes would also of necessity engage them in dialectical thinking, and increases in such thinking should strengthen their argumentative writing" (Hays, Brandt, and Chantry 1988, p. 46).

Another study suggests a strong relationship between relativism and empathy (Benack 1984). The counseling techniques of graduate students classified as "dualistic" or "relativistic" on the basis of interviews conducted at the start of a counseling course revealed that in counseling sessions, dualistic student-counselors failed to focus on the current experiences of the client. In contrast, relativistic student-counselors oriented the conversation toward internal aspects of the client's experience. They used empathic counseling techniques, actively attempting to construct an accurate, flexible model of the client's experience. Relativists were more tentative than dualists, offering hypotheses about the client's concerns and modifying them in response to the client's statements.

The techniques used by the relativistic student-counselors reflect many features of expert problem-solving behavior described in the previous section of this report. They also suggest a genuine attempt to understand the other person, characteristic of connected knowledge, as described by Belenky and associates. Learning to take another person's point of view is important in critical thinking, persuasive writing, and argumentation as well as in counseling.

Mature moral reasoning, which also requires taking a perspective, may depend on epistemological development. A six-year longitudinal study found that reflective judgment interview scores were moderately correlated with a measure of moral development (.48 to .61) (King, Kitchener, and Wood 1985). The level of moral development was found to be "attributable, at least in part, to development of reflective judgment" (p. 9). Similarly, a two-year study of high school students' progress on both moral and epistemological measures found that higher stages of moral development presupposed higher position ratings on Perry's scheme (Clinchy, Lief, and Young 1977). In that study, extraordinarily high levels of both moral and epistemological reasoning were observed in students who were enrolled in a "progressive" high school that emphasized democratic student participation in policy making and active argumentation in classes.

Changing Students' Beliefs about Knowledge

Developmental models help to understand critical thinking as students experience it. Students' resistance to critical thinking frequently arises from one of two fundamental epistemological belief systems: dualism/received knowledge and multiplicity/subjective knowledge. These belief systems are so powerful and pervasive that they can rightly be considered "core misconceptions" comparable in strength to the Aristotelian notions of science identified by cognitive psychologists among college students and other adults. From the perspective of informal logic, dualism and multiplicity may be construed as *fallacies* (distortions of reasoning) of a very high order.

Virtually every decision involved in planning a course can be viewed through an epistemological lens. For example, the choice of a text—and in fact the decision to use a textbook as opposed to primary source material—is one such decision. Textbooks that present subject matter as nonproblematic reinforce dualistic thinking. In contrast, primary documents or textbooks that present controversies within a discipline challenge students to investigate diverse points of view. Moreover, the kinds of assignments, evaluation criteria, and examinations a professor chooses let students know whether they will have to "think" (i.e., be "relativists"), offer opinions (be "multiplists" or "subjectivists"), or simply memorize in the familiar dualistic fashion. The decision to lecture, use discussions, or employ experiential methods like role play or laboratory or field work similarly contributes to the epistemological structure of the course. Finally, the character of discussion in the classroom communicates important information to students about the view of knowledge the course embodies.

A mismatch between students' epistemological beliefs and the developmental challenges of a course can lead to surprising results. For example, an attempt to teach highly "authoritarian" (dualistic) students the techniques of critical thinking resulted in gains on a test of critical thinking, but it also prompted "internecine warfare" in the class. Students sought evidence to "prove" their points and disregarded evidence favoring their opponents' views. They also demanded a great deal of structure from the instructor, a teaching assistant who was unaware that he was involved in an experiment. Two other groups of students, whose beliefs as described by the authors corresponded more closely to epistemological levels 2 and 3, had no difficulty learning the techniques and applying them rationally; all three groups were taught by the same instructor (Stern and Cope 1956, cited in Jacob 1957, p. 74). Students who do not realize that knowledge is contextual may use critical thinking techniques to bolster their preconceived ideas of what is right (Nickerson 1986b). They may also claim that the professor who attempts to teach them to think is neglecting a fundamental responsibility: to present the "facts" of the subject.

Developmentalists hold that beliefs about knowledge can be

influenced toward greater complexity by challenging students' simplistic conceptions while supporting their attempts to manage complexity to the degree necessary to foster intellectual risk taking (Sanford 1966). *Challenges* appeal to what Perry terms "the urge to progress," while *supports* honor "the urge to conserve" or retain one's current identity (Perry 1970, p. 52). Optimal challenge occurs when instruction embodies epistemological assumptions one level beyond the students' present belief system (Hunt 1966; Knefelkamp and Slepitza 1976; Kurfiss 1975; Widick 1975; Widick, Knefelkamp, and Parker 1975; Widick and Simpson 1978). Thus, for students whose beliefs correspond to those of level 1, the optimal challenge is the idea that diverse views can be legitimate. For level 2, the expectation that opinions must have reasons and can be challenged on rational grounds optimally challenges their subjectivist assumptions. At level 3, affirming a position amid uncertainty is a challenge that requires courage and integrity as well as rationality.

What counts as support also differs for students at different developmental levels. Received knowers benefit from affirmation of the worth of their own inner resources. Reassurances and guidelines reduce the risks of openness to new ideas. A cooperative, peer-oriented classroom atmosphere is valued by students in multiplicity, and peers become increasingly important sources of learning as students develop (Baxter-Magolda 1987). Procedural knowers benefit from recognizing that disciplinary methods supplement and enhance their inner voice rather than supplanting or silencing it (Belenky et al. 1986). A caring, interested teacher who respects the student is valued in some form at all levels (Baxter-Magolda 1987). A sense of community with others engaged in a common quest, derived "from reciprocal acts of recognition and confirmation" of the risks students take in caring, provides important support, especially at higher levels (Perry 1970, p. 213).

To provide an "optimal" balance of challenge and support, it helps to have an idea of the developmental levels of students in the course. Formal assessments include the measure of intellectual development (Knefelkamp and Moore n.d.), the measure of epistemological reflection (Baxter-Magolda and Porterfield 1985), and the reflective judgment interview described earlier. Instructors can estimate their students' developmental perspectives using a short questionnaire like the one devised by Ryan (1984a, 1984b) or one tailored to the content of the course (Mortensen and Moreland 1985). A measure under development, called the instructional strategies inventory, provides a profile of students' instructional preferences as a class, which can be compared to the professors' assessment of the developmental requirements of the course (Kurfiss 1987).

Virtually every model for teaching thinking and fostering intellectual development advocates extensive student-teacher and student-student discussion, but engaging students in classroom dialogue is not always easy. Dialogue in college classrooms is scarce; teachers' questions are dominated by requests for factual information (Barnes 1983; Boyer 1987; Hamblen 1984). Class discussions often stay at the level of "quiz shows," "rambling bull" sessions, or "wrangling bull" sessions (Roby 1983, 1985). In quiz shows, students answer information questions posed by the teacher. Quiz shows reinforce dualism and received knowledge. Opinion-sharing conversations are called "rambling bull" sessions. If the discussion leader or a student introduces a "controversial turn" (a question that invites disagreement), the discussion becomes an argument in which participants ardently advocate the correctness of their opinions; this type of dialogue is called a "wrangling bull" session. Bull sessions reinforce multiplicity/subjective knowledge. In these quasi-discussions, no true exchange or thoughtful evaluation of ideas takes place.

True discussions (informational, problematical, dialectical, and reflexive) provide valuable experiences in reasoned discussion of complex, open-ended questions for students in the first three developmental levels. In an informational discussion, the teacher encourages students to speak, defers controversy, and lets students know their ideas will not be evaluated. A "problem-posing" query can shift discussion to consideration of the broader base of information or values needed to address the issue intelligently; this type is a "problematical" discussion. The "devil's advocate" is a request that participants state opposing views accurately and sympathetically. The devil's advocate encourages "dialectical discussion," in which students synthesize diverse opinions into a new formulation of the issue or agree to disagree but with a better understanding of the nature of their differences. Finally, discussion may be "reflexive" in that participants discuss their own discussion in an attempt to learn from the process (Roby 1983, 1985).

By sequencing questions to guide discussion through these four types, the professor provides structure and clarification of divergent views needed by level 1 students. The opportunity to express their opinions, initially without evaluation, supports level 2 students as well. Requests for elaboration step up the challenge of the discussion for all students; use of the devil's advocate "cools down" the conversation, providing reassurance that nobody will be "made wrong." Reflecting on the discussion, perhaps using the categories presented here, enables students to learn about the process of argumentation and encourages them to take greater responsibility for their contribution to the quality of classroom discourse (Roby 1983). Using this model, instruction can cycle through a developmental sequence many times during a semester, allowing students gradually to become more comfortable and more adept in the use of relativistic thinking. (For examples of questions for each form of discussion, see Roby 1983 and 1985, as well as Alvermann, Dillon, and O'Brien 1987 and Dillon 1984).

In any discussion, the professor's responses to students' contributions influence their willingness to contribute further. Effective response strategies include praising and building on students' responses (Smith 1977), directing comments and questions to other students, and remaining silent (Dillon 1984).

Conclusion

Developmental theories describe how students learn to step outside their frame of reference, to recognize that they are reasoning from within a specific context. Understanding students' progressive transformations as knowers enables faculty to appreciate the gradual and often painful path students must tread to recognize the uncertainty of what was once truth for them and to acknowledge legitimacy in perspectives that differ from their own.

To engage students in critical thinking thus calls upon educators to do more than teach the mechanics of analyzing arguments. They must entice students who await "received knowledge" in a dualistic world to entertain the notion that diverse points of view on a subject exist and are legitimate; having achieved this step, they must persuade "subjective knowers" that the existence of inner truth and pluralism does not preclude substantive judgment. They must encourage students to take the point of view of others, even when students object. To intensify students' involvement in learning, they must facilitate integration of students' personal concerns with their quest for deeper knowledge of the subject.

The epistemological journey involved cannot be accomplished with textbook exercises in analysis of arguments. Extended, thoughtfully sequenced discourse about multifaceted issues in a socially supportive but intellectually challenging classroom appears to help, but it carries no guarantees. Development thrives in a richly interactive and personalized environment, a hothouse for intellectual growth. The potential for such growth remains largely untapped in most institutions of higher learning, with the possible exception of small, usually private, residential liberal arts colleges (Boyer 1987; Chickering 1974).

Two significant pedagogical challenges arise from consideration of deliberate developmental education. First is the pressing question of how to increase students' recognition of cultural contexts outside their own experience. Second is the broader question of how education for critical thinking influences ethical reasoning and action.

Expanding contextual awareness

While reading and classroom discussion can shake some students loose from simplistic thinking and ethnocentric biases, real-world experiences may be a still more potent source of decentering. Within the confines of the classroom, much may be accomplished by having students reflect on the meaning of their own day-to-day experiences, for example, work and relationships to authority, using material generated by the students (Shor 1980, 1987) or love and loneliness as illustrated in classic texts (Gamson and Associates 1984; see especially pp. 96–101). Field experiences linked with instruction provide a bridge between concrete and abstract learning (Hursh and Borzak 1979; Wulff and Nyquist 1988).

Beyond the classroom, internships that take students into cultural settings different from their own (preferably both to live and work) have been a central feature of education at some institutions, most notably Antioch College, which requires students to alternate between on-campus study quarters and cooperative work experiences away from campus. Multicultural experiences close to home can often be arranged, particularly on urban campuses. Experiences abroad are a traditional and respected means of awakening students to the diversity of human culture and contexts.

Critical thinking, values, and action

Educators are generally reluctant to encourage moral and ethical deliberation in their classrooms (Morrill 1980; Scriven

1980), yet it is difficult to avoid questions of values when teaching for critical thinking. Frequently, value questions are viewed as extraneous to instruction and may be brushed aside when they do arise. For example, students in a marketing class began a case analysis by discussing strategies for marketing birth control pills in an underdeveloped Catholic country but ended up debating the morality of such activity. The "section man" intervened, saying that the discussion was "not appropriate" in a marketing class, where the central problem of the case is how the company should distribute its product. As a consequence, "no further 'social-ethical' questions were raised" in the class that semester (Christensen 1987, p. 186).

No context (even that of the supposedly "value-neutral" scientific method) is free of value assumptions, but the place of values and ethical deliberations in the curriculum is problematic (see Collins 1983 for discussion). Ethical questions arise "at *the margins between* different professional enterprises or at *the points where* professional and private lives meet and overlap" (Toulmin, Rieke, and Janik 1979, p. 310). If instruction in critical thinking is to influence behavior, it must address these points of intersection. Teaching students technical skills to achieve goals while excluding discussion of the values those goals imply reduces critical thinking to a narrow set of technical skills, violating a fundamental purpose of instruction in critical thinking.

Conversations about ethical questions call upon skills that many faculty are not accustomed to using in the classroom (Morrill 1980). Deliberations about how an individual, group, or nation *ought* to act on matters of personal and social importance, however, give purpose to learning and energize class discussions. Guided discussion of moral dilemmas and reflection on self in relation to others pays off in growth toward contextual moral reasoning (Schlaefli, Rest, and Thoma 1985). Educators' reluctance to engage students in ethical deliberations may account for the finding that moral development lags behind intellectual development. Under different educational circumstances, contextual reasoning in both the moral and intellectual domain might be more common and more closely intertwined.

When they avoid such deliberations, educators widen the chasm between "school learning" and "real life." They reduce the probability that students' *knowledge* will influence their personal and professional *actions* toward rational, socially responsible ends. Education for critical thinking, viewed developmentally, challenges students, but it also challenges faculty: to extend their own intellectual inquiries beyond traditional disciplinary boundaries, to make room for extended inquiries in their teaching, and to encourage students to consider critical issues arising from the subject matter of the course. To the extent that a wider, developmental view of critical thinking is adopted, the prospects for greater intellectual and ethical maturity of college graduates will be greatly improved.

TEACHING CRITICAL THINKING IN THE DISCIPLINES

Critical thinking can now be seen as the product of knowledge, skills, cognitive and metacognitive processes, an epistemological stance, and the purposes of the learner. In the classroom, these elements ebb and flow, become dominant and recede, depending on the agenda set by the teacher and the kind of community that develops among the students.

This section describes classroom approaches to critical thinking as reported, for the most part, by the teachers who designed them. Science, mathematics, and engineering projects emphasize solving problems; they illustrate methods based primarily on cognitive research. Developmental themes dominate in the humanities projects. Projects in the social sciences and teacher education draw from all three theoretical frameworks.

Some of the courses described here were designed on the basis of principles inferred from theory and research. Others were not, although they can be understood in terms of one or more of the three frameworks described here. Theory and research are not prescriptive; they do not dictate instructional methods. They are a resource for thinking about how students interpret their learning experiences and how the classroom might be organized to achieve particular educational goals. The diverse projects described below testify to the truism that when it comes to designing instruction, there is no one right answer. Some "answers," however, increase rather than restrict students' possibilities for growth and are therefore "better." Educating for intellectual growth is the unifying theme of the examples described here.

The characteristically American view that there is not "time" to allow students to think has probably done considerable damage to learning and appreciating science in the United States.

The Sciences, Mathematics, and Engineering

Science educators have taken a number of steps to counteract the "novice" problem-solving strategies of their students. Instruction in problem solving, formal reasoning, and scientific experimentation can be integrated with learning content, as the following examples illustrate.

Prefreshman skill development

Metacognition in reading and problem solving and formal operational reasoning are the target skills in a prefreshman program at Xavier University called SOAR (Stress on Analytical Reasoning). The course is intensive: five weeks, five hours a day plus study time. Classes are very small and staff thoroughly trained. This program pays off for students in terms of completion of a science degree and enrollment in medical school (Carmichael 1982).

To develop metacognitive skills, students use the "Thinking-Aloud Pair Problem Solving" (TAPPS) method, taking turns verbalizing their thoughts while reading or solving progressively more difficult problems. Weekly team competitions foster cooperative learning and extra studying. Reading comprehension and PSAT scores increase as a result of the program (Lochhead and Whimbey 1987; Whimbey et al. 1980; Whimbey and Lochhead 1979).

To develop formal operational reasoning skills, students spent three hours a day completing laboratory exercises using the "learning cycle" format (Karplus 1974). In the laboratory, the student/faculty ratio was held to roughly 7:1. Faculty were trained to respond to students' questions and written work with questions to promote independent thinking. The program successfully cultivated formal reasoning skills in students who lacked them when they began (Carmichael et al. 1980). The learning cycle method was so successful that faculty introduced it into the general chemistry laboratory program. Standard verification-type labs were replaced by problem-based labs; students were encouraged to discuss conflicting results. The revised labs enhanced formal reasoning skills with no decrease in performance on final examination practicals. Attendance in the learning cycle sections was superior to that in the traditional section, and students were uniformly positive in their ratings of the course (Ryan, Robinson, and Carmichael 1980).

As noted in the section on historical background, discussed earlier, the ADAPT program successfully used learning cycles in many disciplines (philosophy, English, history, algebra, anthropology, and others). ADAPT students demonstrated significant improvement in both formal reasoning and critical thinking skills (Tomlinson-Keasey and Eisert 1978).

Integrated science

Matter and energy are the major content themes of an interdisciplinary general education science course at Alverno College. The course aims to develop skills in scientific reasoning (observation, recognizing patterns, raising questions, formulating hypotheses, and designing experiments) and to foster a critical attitude toward popular scientific literature (Loacker et al. 1984). Students work in pairs, thinking aloud while solving problems in a guided sequence from instructor-posed problems to design of experiments to test student-generated hypotheses. Peer questioning and articulation of reasoning processes are emphasized throughout the course. Students report formally to the class on both the processes and outcomes of their "investigative learning" laboratory projects. Having conducted their own scientific inquiry, students recognize the value of scientific analysis in many aspects of their lives and lose their initial habit of "being intimidated by science" (Loacker et al. 1984, p. 52).

Biology

Basic skills of scientific reasoning and methodology are the aim of a year-long lower-division course for biology majors at a two-year college (Logan 1987). Target skills are description and definition, application, deductive inference, and induction. The professor defines these skills and illustrates how they are used or misused; students' thinking is described and evaluated in terms of the skill model. Students also learn the scientific method: how to formulate a hypothesis, analyze and interpret experimental data, construct models, identify alternative conclusions that might suggest further investigations, and consider wider applications of results. Critical thinking skills are also tested on both essay and multiple-choice examinations (see Logan 1987 for examples of test items).

Learning by doing and talking in science

The methods described here stimulate science learning by having students *do* science and reason with scientific concepts rather than by hearing about it and completing formulaic laboratory exercises. Pure "discovery" methods are rejected in favor of systematic guided learning experiences that nonetheless put students in charge and engage scientific reasoning. High levels of peer interaction are a common theme. These methods allow students to figure out scientific processes and concepts in their own way, at their own pace. Traditional methods, with their excessive and premæ ● re emphasis on scientific terminology, often preclude development of genuine understanding (Lochhead 1979). The characteristically American view that there is not "time" to allow students to think has probably done considerable damage to learning and appreciating science in the United States. The same can be said of mathematics.

Mathematics

Metacognitive skills are the primary focus of a course in mathematical problem solving taught by Schoenfeld (1985a, 1985b).

Students learn to make conscious, justifiable decisions in the process of solving problems. In class, students solve "reasonably difficult" problems that may take as long as 50 minutes. When working with the whole class, Schoenfeld takes on the role of metacognitive monitor. He raises questions about suggestions students offer for solving the problem and encourages them to identify and evaluate several approaches before they try one. After five minutes or so of working on a solution, he asks them to evaluate their progress. Even after a problem is solved, the class goes back to alternatives to see where they lead. He does *not* try to prevent students from going off in an incorrect direction "as long as the decision [is] reasonably made" (1985b, p. 373).

When students work in small groups, the professor functions as a "roving 'consultant' "; responsibility for the role of "external manager" shifts to the students (1985b, p. 374). A poster on the classroom wall proclaims three key questions as a reminder to students:

> *What (exactly) are you doing?*
> *(Can you describe it precisely?)*
> *Why are you doing it?*
> *(How does it fit into the solution?)*
> *How does it help you?*
> *(What will you do with the outcome when you obtain it?)*
> (1985a, p. 222; 1985b, p. 374).

When the course begins, students cannot answer these questions. Upon completing the course, students spend much more time planning their solution strategies and monitor their progress more consistently. Students who complete the course also become more like experts in their categorization of problems, although it is not an explicit focus of the course (Schoenfeld and Herrmann 1982).

Schoenfeld claims that traditional education in mathematics creates and reinforces students' view of themselves as nonquantitative thinkers (Schoenfeld 1983a, 1985a, 1985b). Mathematics instruction has also been criticized for its use of exercises "unrelated to the math one actually uses in everyday life" (Frankenstein 1987, p. 194). When mathematics is taught in an authoritarian manner and problems are irrelevant to real life, students learn to be intimidated by numbers.

Statistics

Students often believe that statistics are "objective." Drawing on the work of Freire (e.g., Freire 1985), Frankenstein (1987) describes a course on statistics for the social sciences in which students learn to question this belief. By investigating the data on which statistics are based, they learn to recognize social biases in "official" statistics used to justify decisions of major corporations or the federal government. For example, how are unemployment data gathered? What distinguishes "welfare" from "tax subsidies" in governmental budget reports? Learning to answer such questions counteracts uncritical acceptance of quantitative information.

Chemical engineering

Real-world problem solving is the target intellectual skill of an introductory chemical engineering course (Wales 1979). The model developed for this course has been successfully adapted in other disciplines where complex problem solving is important, for example, geography (Martinson 1981) and industrial psychology (Miller 1981).

Students in the course learn a systematic approach for thinking about problems and making decisions. The model, called guided design, slows down the decision process by having students work through a series of steps in teams, pausing after each step to compare their results with those of an imaginary team working on the same problem. The imaginary team is *not* a group of experts who have "found the right answer." Their "reports" can be incorporated into the team's work or disregarded.

Students who completed exercises in guided design during their first year in chemical engineering were more likely than nonparticipants to complete the full engineering program, and their grade point averages in subsequent courses were higher than those of previous classes (Wales 1979). Participants also showed gains on a test of decision making, while students who were instructed in the model but did not complete the exercises showed no comparable gains (Hursh et al. n.d.).

Problem-solving skill courses

Transferable problem-solving skills are the goal of an interdisciplinary course taught by a host of faculty at UCLA since 1969. The course, which is housed in the School of Engineer-

ing, arose from concerns about the increasing need for techno-
logical literacy (Rubinstein 1980).

The 10-week course emphasizes both conceptual foundations
of problem solving and specific problem-solving techniques,
such as tree diagramming, problem representation, and probability. Students also examine their problem-solving style. Decision making and values are also emphasized in the course,
which takes an interdisciplinary approach. In addition to working on problems in the text (*Patterns of Problem Solving*—
Rubinstein 1975; see also Rubinstein 1986), students complete
a project of their own choosing. A peer teaching program,
using trained peer teachers, supplements class instruction. Although the course has not been extensively evaluated, Ruben-
stein reports a small study demonstrated significant gains on an
intelligence test for participants in a similar course at St. Louis
University (Bartlett, cited in Rubinstein 1980, pp. 35–36).

The Humanities

Courses in the humanities aim to teach students to find meaning in human creations and to articulate the basis for their responses. Developmental issues often surface in these courses.
Some students fail to understand that texts or works of art must
be "interpreted." Viewed developmentally, these responses are
those of "received knowers" (Belenky et al. 1986) or "dualists" (Perry 1970). Other students believe that interpretation is
"purely" subjective and that judgment is therefore inappro-
priate. They are "subjective knowers" or "multiplists." Mature appreciation of the humanities recognizes that while interpretations and judgments differ, some are more firmly grounded
in the work than others and hence more "plausible" if not
more "true" or "correct."

Interpretation or evaluation may *begin* with personal responses to a work, but students must learn to articulate the *basis* for their response by analyzing the work using methods
appropriate to the medium. This is the task of "procedural
knowing" (Belenky et al. 1986). That analysis suggests that
students may approach works in the humanities either by "connecting" with the intent of the artist or author or by distancing
themselves from it, using analytical techniques ("separate
knowledge").

Literature

To encourage students to connect with literary works, they
were asked to create metaphors to describe a character or other

aspect of the text (Muellerleile 1986). The researcher alternated the assignment on metaphors with assignments requiring traditional analysis of the works (e.g., describe a character and specify facts from the text that support the description). Comparing results of the two methods, she concluded that metaphors fostered better understanding of the texts, greater integration of personal perspectives into students' experience of the work, better writing, and "a new kind of intellectual excitement, challenge, and pleasure" (p. 31). The indirect, "connecting" strategy of finding metaphors thus engaged students in thinking about the works more fully than did analytical questions usually associated with critical thinking.

Journals provide another method to encourage students to connect with works of literature, art, music, or philosophy. In an introductory poetry course, VanDeWeghe (1986) posed problems for students to address in journal entries. As the term progressed, they began to pose and respond to problems they discovered in their reading. Writing often fostered insights and fresh interpretations of the material. Students overcame their initial reluctance to explore poetry in this way and developed confidence in their ability to "make sense" of literary works.

Leahy (1985) offers a model for grading to counteract multiplistic students' concerns about "subjectivity" or instructors' "bias" in grading critical thinking assignments. In his literature course, grading was based exclusively on journals in which students responded to course material that was also discussed in class. With assistance from the class, he devised grading criteria that included a minimum number of entries (about five per week, about 300 words per entry); use of "a variety of strategies for learning: summary, questioning, speculation, synthesis, problem solving, and relating of subject matter to the writer's prior knowledge and experience"; and reference to specific details in the works studied (p. 110). Students' grades were based on responses from five peers, a self-evaluation, and the professor's final judgment. Students were realistic in assigning their own grades, and disagreements about grades were not an issue in the course. Journals should be checked frequently to monitor students' progress and to foster accountability.

Professors' responses to students' writing communicate interest; they can also be tailored to "optimally" challenge and support students' growth. Recognizing developmental assumptions implicit in students' work, the professor can offer suggestions and raise questions that encourage the student to think in new channels, while supporting the progress evident in what they have accomplished. (See Schmidt and Davison 1983 for guidelines for developmental responding.)

Philosophy

In philosophy classes, professors often encounter students who subscribe to dualism/received knowledge. These students place primary value on knowledge received directly from the authority in the course; they want the professor to provide *the* interpretation of texts or *the* synthesis of historical "facts." Many students embrace dogmatic rules about ethical and moral situations (Riordan 1986). For such students, the questioning of truth and values that is the core of philosophy is challenging and, for many, disturbing and even frightening, especially when it directly confronts their core values (Reinsmith 1987).

Rather than attack dogmatic thinking (and by implication, his students' core values) directly, Riordan assigns students reading that

> . . . *somehow helps them experience the limitations of their dogmatism. John Stuart Mill's essay, "On the Subjection of Women," for example, does an excellent job of illustrating how narrow, unquestioned thinking has led to the oppression of women and others. When students begin to see that dogmatism has affected their lives [his students are all women] in rather profound and sometimes tragic ways, they are more likely to raise questions about their own points of view and be open to thinkers who do the same* (Riordan 1986, p. 22).

This indirect, supportive approach enables students to maintain their dignity and self-respect, while freeing them to acknowledge legitimacy in ideas different from their own. From this foundation, they can approach the ideas and interpretive frameworks and methods of philosophy more receptively.

Developing transferable critical thinking skills is the goal of one humanities course (Wolters 1986). To transfer understanding from familiar situations to new ones, students must be able to perceive commonalities in diverse situations, recognize the ways in which rules or principles are modified in specific situations, and understand a situation from many perspectives. Wolters uses assessment to foster these abilities, reflecting a theme in Alverno's institutional approach (described later). Students in his ethics course study six theorists. At the beginning of the course, they write an essay describing how they would respond to a dramatic situation that poses an ethical dilemma. The same situation reappears on each examination in the course; each time, students describe the situation as it would be viewed from the perspective of the ethicist just studied. They also respond to the analysis. Students' essays show continued growth throughout the term, especially when they are informed that the question will be repeated. The method probably works best when the units of the course are relatively similar so that a common problem can be identified for repeated use (Wolters 1986).

Foreign languages

Instruction in foreign languages opens the door to appreciation of cultural differences, freeing students from the bondage of ethnocentrism. Trends in language instruction, however, have led many educators to teach from "culturally sanitized" texts chosen or rewritten to reflect theoretical concepts about the level of difficulty students can handle. The result, in one view, is that "not meaningfulness but sentence length and syllable counts become the decisive factors" in assembling anthologies for foreign language instruction (Swaffer 1986, p. 80).

Deploring the increasing emphasis on mechanical aspects of instruction in a second language, one instructor uses active approaches that help students understand the culture while they use the language in meaningful ways (Terrio 1986). For example, students keep a simulated travel diary and hold a mock press conference. The instructor also advocates using approaches similar to those used in process-centered English composition courses. In her French courses, students use prewriting, sentence-combining exercises (in which students construct complex sentences from a given set of short declarative sentences), critical reading of texts, peer exchange and review of work in progress on compositions in the language, sequenced assignments, and journals. Techniques like these, which require skills of inquiry and collaboration among students, are highly effective in teaching first-language writing skills (Hillocks 1984, 1986). Immersing students in realistic language use enhances the cross-cultural benefit of language study.

Art criticism

Teachers' questioning techniques determine the critical thinking skills students use in a classroom. One instructor reviews literature on questioning and demonstrates its relevance in teaching art criticism (Hamblen 1984). She contends that in art classes, as in other disciplines, low-level questions that emphasize factual recall are the norm. She points out that formats for art criticism require "ever-increasing complex levels of thinking that closely parallel the categories of many learning models," generally beginning with description, analysis, and interpretation and culminating in an evaluation or judgment (p. 19). These categories can be used to guide questioning in "art dialogues" between students and teachers. Probing questions to stimulate elaboration of students' ideas should also be used. The instructor notes that students need time to respond to questions and urges teachers to encourage *students* to ask high-level questions. Her sequenced approach guides students toward judgment, while strengthening their understanding of the work to be evaluated.

Interdisciplinary study of literature

Fostering progress on the Perry scheme was the deliberate aim of an interdisciplinary course, "Themes in Human Identity," which combined theoretical perspectives in psychology with the study of identity in literary works (Knefelkamp 1974; Stephenson and Hunt 1977; Widick, Knefelkamp, and Parker 1975). In one study, two sections of the course were created, one for dualistic students and another for relativists. Instruction was organized to provide optimal levels of diversity, experience, structure, and personalism, using the developmental design model described earlier in this report. For example, in the study of *Zorba the Greek*, characters' conflicting world views offered one kind of challenge; analyzing characters using all three of the psychological frameworks studied offered another. Students were persistently asked, "Are there other ways to explain that?" Journals, interviews, class debates, and fantasy immersion in characters provided direct experience of diversity with the intent of fostering empathy. A personal atmosphere and the instructor's control of course-related decisions provided support. In the relativistic "intervention," students confronted the issue of commitment in the literature studied and had control over decisions, such as when to turn in journals.

Students in the section that "matched" their developmental needs made significant progress (approaching a full stage) on Perry's scheme, while those who were "mismatched" progressed less (Widick, Knefelkamp, and Parker 1975). A modification of the dualistic intervention was replicated in a second course, this time with two control groups for comparison. Students in the developmentally designed course progressed, on the average, nearly a full position on a Perry scheme measure. Students in a humanities course taught by a supportive instructor progressed less than half a position; students in a traditional English course progressed roughly one-tenth of a position (Stephenson and Hunt 1977).

Instruction in critical thinking in the humanities involves extensive use of discussion and writing about topics that can be understood from many perspectives. The problems posed to students give purpose to their reading. Attention to students' developmental needs is a factor in the success of several courses described here.

Understanding the grading criteria used to evaluate their work is a primary task for students learning to think critically.

Social Sciences
Subject matter in the social sciences is problematic and often controversial, offering numerous opportunities for critical thinking.

Research methods
In psychology, scientific methods are an important tool for critical thinking. In a fourth-year honors research methods course, psychology majors experience critical thinking in a realistic context: the submission of research results to a "journal." The course simulates three aspects of academic research: collaboration, criticism, and constraints upon acceptance of completed work. Students share work in progress in seminars beginning early in the course; peer questions and criticisms provide practice in formulating, evaluating, and defending ideas. Faculty in the department review papers for the course. Strict deadlines increase the realism of the simulation. About half of these papers result in conference papers or publications (Furedy and Furedy 1979).

History
Understanding history requires the ability to perceive multiple causes and to interpret historical accounts. History is often taught, however, as if it were a straightforward record of well-documented events. An extended simulation used to teach contemporary world history challenged students' simplistic ideas about history. The simulation approach was compared with the traditional lecture method to test the hypothesis that students who had not achieved formal operational reasoning might bene-

fit from the concrete experiences provided by a simulation game (Laveault and Corbeil 1985).

The game invited students to "participate" in the international politics of the first half of this century. Teams of students acted as leaders of various countries. The instructor provided scenarios that students responded to with plans or "orders." Students evaluated the outcomes of their plans in writing. The game stimulated motivation beyond the demands of the course, eventually taking on characteristics of true international politics. Students held meetings outside of class to plan their strategies, negotiated with and spied on other teams, and conducted library research to devise winning strategies. The simulation gave students an experiential basis for discussing important but potentially abstract political issues, such as alternatives to warfare. On a measure of factual knowledge, students in the simulation scored as well as students in a traditional version of the course. The course facilitated students' ability to identify the context of historical documents and was effective for students at both the concrete and formal operational levels (Laveault and Corbeil 1985).

Political science
Countering ethnocentrism is the goal of a political science course in which students study multinational perspectives on an issue. For example, they learn about the Cuban missile crisis from the American, Soviet, and Cuban points of view. As they study each perspective, they are asked to "believe" it insofar as possible. After they have heard all three views, they evaluate them in class discussion and writing. This approach lets students experience the legitimacy of alternative interpretations without requiring them to give up their own position (Freie 1987). Having three points of view avoids polarization of the issues, which, from an epistemological angle, suggests a useful way to counteract dualistic responses.

Social sciences
Analytical skills, recognition of social patterns, and an understanding of how social systems shape behavior are the goals of the introductory social sciences course at Alverno (Loacker et al. 1984). Students reflect on their experience in educational systems, discovering patterns (such as social hierarchies) that have influenced them and that reflect concepts used by social scientists to understand experience. Having gained an experien-

tial foundation and a working vocabulary of principles, students spend five weeks in group work identifying a social problem and developing their own approach to it. They become a "small-scale social system" (p. 66), which itself becomes an object of study in the course. Journals, readings, drawings, and class discussions provide multiple opportunities for expression and learning in the course.

Psychology

To foster critical thinking skills in psychology, Halonen (1985, 1986) offers a model developed by a team of psychologists from several campuses. According to the model, "discrepant events" introduced in a course challenge students' "personal theories" (schemas or "stories" that explain particular phenomena), motivating them to resolve the discrepancy by revising the theory. The model is illustrated in a variety of psychology courses.

For example, to practice application of knowledge and both divergent and critical thinking, students in a course on psychological testing design a simple test of intelligence and test it on 10 people. Discussion of the results and problems, both procedural and ethical, reveals grounds for skepticism about such tests. The exercise, which is especially discrepant (surprising) when introduced on the first day of class, provides an experiential foundation for subsequent conceptual learning (Halonen 1986, pp. 77–79).

Social issues

Students learn to integrate conflicting information to construct a reasonable position on social issues in a method called "cooperative controversy" (Johnson and Johnson 1985). Students study issues in groups of fours. Pairs within each group study materials favoring opposing points of view, then present their findings to each other. They then switch sides, study additional materials, and make a second presentation. Team members arrive at a consensus on the topic and write a report representing the group's views. Finally, students write individual reports arguing for their position on the issue.

Students who learned in this fashion incorporated more opposing ideas into their final arguments and more frequently engaged in active search for additional information on the topic, when compared with groups taught in a debate team format or through individualized instruction (Johnson and Johnson 1985).

The method was tested on middle-school children, but it offers both supportive and challenging elements for dualistic and multiplistic students in lower-division courses. (See Cohen 1986, Feichtner and Davis 1984–85, and Johnson et al. 1984 for suggestions for organizing group work.)

Anthropology

Alerting students to the influence of an observer's frame of reference is the aim of a unit in anthropology designed for high school students (Swartz 1986). The teacher provides a visual model of the concept, "frame of reference," showing how it influences the choice of subject, information seen as relevant, guiding hypothesis, and use of evidence. Students then study two anthropological descriptions of women in !Kung society, answer questions on male-female dominance in each account, and identify descriptive terms used by the authors. In comparing the two accounts, some discrepancies can be understood easily, but others cannot, leading students to the question, "So whom do we believe?" (Swartz 1986, p. 116). The frame-of-reference model is reintroduced to guide the remaining discussion. Support derives from the realization that some facts can be agreed upon, but the instructor does not seek to reduce the complexity of the question. She does, however, emphasize the model as a tool for understanding rather than cynically "unmasking" an author's biases.

Field work

A model for field-based courses was shown to foster relativistic thinking (Hursh and Borzak 1979). Students in two internship programs in community service agencies wrote papers, completed readings in research and theory, kept field journals, and attended weekly seminars to discuss their learning. Comparison of pre- and postseminar assessments revealed increased flexibility in taking different points of view, less separation of academic life from the "real world," and more realistic views of possibilities for change in organizations. And some students began to recognize the value of course work outside their professional area of interest.

The examples described here illustrate the use of controversy, problems, and students' experiences to foster involvement in learning. Writing, work in small groups, and extended discussion are common features of these courses. These courses are developmentally "optimal" for dualist and multiplist students because they invite exploration of multiple points of view and support students as they formulate their own views.

Teacher Education

Students in teacher education frequently share the "common sense" view that "experience is the best teacher." They see nothing wrong with the fact that teachers learn primarily by doing, unsupported by the elaborate socialization and training required of other, higher-status professionals (Zeuli and Buchmann 1986). They are often highly context bound, attending college and planning to teach in their home state.

At Michigan State University, two goals were identified for the required social foundations course: to broaden students' understanding of the context of teaching and to increase their capacity for reflective rather than habitual practice based on personal inclination and experience as a student (Zeuli and Buchmann 1986). Students studied research and theory relevant to these goals (using Lortie's *Schoolteacher*). They compared teacher socialization to that of other professions, and they examined instances of satisfaction in teaching and learning through interviews and personal accounts. Although students recognized the personal nature of both professional preparation and practice in education, they failed to recognize the limitations of self-socialization and habitual practice.

Developing the capacity for critical reflection through student teaching is the goal of an inquiry-oriented program at the University of Wisconsin–Madison. Three levels of reflection are identified: technical competence, which is the efficient application of known methods to achieve unquestioned ends in teaching; analytical practice, in which the consequences of teaching actions are assessed; and critical reflection, which examines social and moral implications of both ends and means within an acknowledged cultural context. The program supplements traditional student teaching experience with an inquiry project, journals, a reflective seminar, and supervisory conferences (Zeichner and Liston 1987). An important element of the program is "respect for cultural diversity" (p. 37). Students are encouraged to evaluate curricular materials for cultural bias and modify them when necessary.

Evaluation of the program indicates that students do not change levels but become more articulate about whatever perspective they held when they entered the program. The program "stems the onrushing move toward a more custodial view'' that frequently develops during student teaching (p. 36). The impact of the program may be more visible as the students progress in their careers (Zeichner and Liston 1987).

Several reasons have been offered for the limited influence of the program (Zeichner and Liston 1987). First, the students' technical orientation fosters resistance to reflection, which is seen as conflicting with time spent on ''the more important tasks of applying and demonstrating knowledge and skills'' (p. 41). Time pressures on faculty in the program also limit the development of close supervisory relationships that might have enhanced the program's impact. Finally, the context of student teaching does not encourage critical analysis, as criticism on the part of the student could easily threaten the supervising teacher and damage the students' chances for a favorable evaluation.

Two courses illustrate the use of controversy, writing, and work in small groups to help students understand the nature of evidence and argument in addressing educational issues. In a research design course based on Freire's pedagogical concepts, students reflect on readings in structured journals. In small groups, they debate issues based on the material. A formal evaluation of the course is planned; students' informal responses to the course have been consistently positive (Martuza 1987).

An introductory course in educational foundations, designed and evaluated using Perry's model, also uses controversy to stimulate contextual reasoning about dilemmas in educational practice (Mortensen and Moreland 1985). Students analyze the role of school in society by studying selected issues (e.g., compulsory education) represented in articles, survey data, historical material, and information on laws and court cases included in a text developed by a faculty team. Students write papers in which they consider evidence for competing positions on the issues. The writing component ''help[s] students clarify their thinking and [gives] invaluable feedback to faculty about student progress in critical thinking,'' as well as holding students accountable for ideas expressed less formally in class discussion (pp. 88–89).

The course apparently provided an optimal match for the primarily multiplistic students who completed it. A sample of 100 students were pre- and posttested on a paper-and-pencil measure based on Perry's model. In this measure, which is based on Kitchener and King's reflective judgment interview format, students explained how they would resolve questions about testing practices and early schooling. The measure was scored using criteria developed at Alverno College (Mentkowski, Moeser, and Strait 1983). Students progressed from predominantly multiplistic to predominantly relativistic responses to the questions. The measure designed for this study provides a good example of how developmental assessment can be tailored to reflect discipline-specific content, increasing the match between measures of evaluation and instruction.

The apparent success of the course may be attributable to the course designers' use of the developmental challenge-and-support model targeted toward multiplistic students, as well as to their choice of a context-specific (and therefore relatively sensitive) evaluation instrument. Providing many experiences of this sort, beginning early in the education curriculum as well as in other courses, might enhance teacher education students' progress toward critical reflection.

Evaluation in Critical Thinking Courses
Evaluating students' work in courses that require critical thinking involves qualitative judgment by the professor. For dualistic and multiplistic students in the course, who do not yet understand the evaluative process, qualitative judgments appear subjective. They may believe they are being graded on "mere opinions" and that matters such as style, clarity, or agreement with the professor's opinion are the primary grading "criteria."

Understanding the grading criteria used to evaluate their work is a primary task for students learning to think critically. As a first step, grading criteria must be made explicit. The criteria should indicate the relative importance of factors such as accuracy and quantity of factual information, "balance" in presenting several points of view, or use of an organizing claim and supporting evidence.

But stating criteria is only a starting point, because students (especially those "in" multiplicity/subjective knowledge) will argue that "it's just a matter of opinion whether the criteria have been met." To make the criteria meaningful and credible to students, the professor may find it necessary to illustrate their application to specific examples of students' work. A guided discussion of good and not-so-good examples of student-produced arguments helps to make the grounds for the professor's judgment explicit to students. Students can also work in groups to evaluate examples produced by their predecessors in the class, then discuss their group judgments and rationale as a class. The professor can provide the criteria or help students generate them by pointing out the reasons they use to judge the work of others. An approach similar to that used in "holistic scoring" of essays can be used to involve students in applying or developing criteria (White 1984, 1985). In a sociology course requiring several critical thinking assignments, students rated class activities directed at clarifying both the process and the criteria for critical thinking assignments most helpful (Pittendrigh and Jobes 1984).

When students participate in development of grading criteria, they are more likely to understand and accept those criteria. Leahy's approach to evaluation in his journal-based literature course (1985), described earlier, exemplifies joint development of criteria for evaluation. Such methods invite students to be responsible for and committed to meeting the demands of the course, while helping them develop skills needed to participate in the "community of scholars."

Common Features of Critical Thinking Courses in the Disciplines

The methods presented here illustrate disciplinary diversity but also reveal a common pedagogical vocabulary for teaching critical thinking. In each case, the professor establishes an agenda that includes learning to think about subject matter. Students are active, involved, consulting and arguing with each other, and responsible for their own learning.

Several principles can be extracted from this brief review of teaching practices that support critical thinking.

1. Critical thinking is a learnable skill; the instructor and peers are resources in developing critical thinking skills.
2. Problems, questions, or issues are the point of entry into the subject and a source of motivation for sustained inquiry.
3. Successful courses balance challenges to think critically with support tailored to students' developmental needs.
4. Courses are assignment centered rather than text and lecture centered. Goals, methods, and evaluation emphasize using content rather than simply acquiring it.
5. Students are required to formulate and justify their ideas in writing or other appropriate modes.
6. Students collaborate to learn and to stretch their thinking,

for example, in pair problem solving and small group work.

7. Several courses, particularly those that teach problem-solving skills, nurture students' metacognitive abilities.

8. The developmental needs of students are acknowledged and used as information in the design of the course. Teachers in these courses make standards explicit and then help students learn how to achieve them.

A single course can influence students' use of thinking skills and may increase epistemological sophistication in a restricted domain. Intellectual maturity, however, requires many experiences investigating subjects from several perspectives and formulating a personal perspective on the subject in writing. Campuswide attention to students' intellectual development will accelerate students' escape from the confines of dualism and the illusory freedom of multiplicity. The next section describes institutional-level efforts to achieve this goal.

INSTITUTIONAL ISSUES AND APPROACHES

While individual faculty frequently emphasize critical thinking in their courses, students' thinking abilities will remain limited unless faculty combine forces to cultivate thinking skills deliberately throughout the curriculum. In recognition, many institutions have identified critical thinking as a collegewide responsibility. Using approaches suited to their respective organizational cultures and students' characteristics, they are demonstrating what can be accomplished when a common faculty concern becomes an institutional project.

Student's thinking abilities will remain limited unless faculty combine forces to cultivate thinking skills deliberately throughout the curriculum.

This section reviews institutional approaches to critical thinking, illustrating how several institutions have used critical thinking as an organizing theme for curricular and instructional innovation. The review first describes several curricular approaches to the development of skill in critical thinking on a continuum from single courses to curriculumwide integration. The section then describes organizational strategies for developing critical thinking programs and identifies characteristics of current programs.

Curricular Approaches

Critical thinking skills can be formally introduced into a curriculum in a single course, in an integrated freshman-year program, or in a program that spans the undergraduate curriculum.

Freshman course

Many institutions offer a single course to teach students the basic skills of critical thinking. Such courses are designed for freshmen and are sometimes required or offered as an alternative in a freshman core program. They generally focus on skills of argument. In some cases, critical thinking and writing skills are combined in a single course.

These courses are structured in a variety of ways, reflecting each institution's concern with particular aspects of critical thinking. For example, SUNY–Buffalo offers a three-credit course based on the methodology of "Learning to Learn." Stressing methods of disciplinary inquiry, the course uses assignments drawn from students' other courses to promote transfer of reasoning skills to a variety of contexts. Clayton State College offers a basic course emphasizing cognitive processes and focusing on two kinds of critical thinking: for solving structured problems, the course teaches problem-solving and decision-making skills; for addressing "contemplative" or more open-ended problems, the course teaches skills of inquiry.

(See Carpenter and Doig 1988 for evaluation criteria and a brief course description.) Like many institutions that have become conscious of the need for explicit attention to critical thinking, the faculty at Clayton State plans to implement critical thinking in courses across the discipline.

In the early 1980s, faculty at SUNY–Fredonia developed a freshman-year program, the General Liberal Education Program (GLEP), which included a course on analytical thinking using methods of informal logic described earlier in this report. The program also included a freshman orientation course and symposia designed to help students integrate their learning experiences through interdisciplinary discussion of current issues and problems. Experience with this program led faculty to realize the "primacy of reasoning, its intimate involvement in reading and writing, and *the inadequacy of a single course devoted openly to the subject*" [of reasoning] (Amiran 1986, p. 4, emphasis added). As a result, the faculty designed a curriculum-wide, developmentally structured general education program (described below) and phased out the GLEP.

Developing a single introductory course is perhaps the least complicated institutional strategy to implement—and in many cases may also be the best place to begin. This approach may lead to complacency, however, if faculty assume the "problem" of students' poor reasoning is being "taken care of" by whoever offers the course. In many institutions, the weight of preparatory instruction in thinking as well as writing is carried by the English department in the freshman composition program. Experience with that structure has led to the realization that wider participation by faculty is needed for writing skills to flourish—hence the growing number of "writing across the curriculum" programs nationally. Faculty response at SUNY–Fredonia and at Clayton State College illustrates that a parallel case can be made for the teaching of reasoning. Involving faculty in designing an introductory critical thinking course offers a way to promote understanding of critical thinking and ultimately to stimulate faculty to incorporate critical thinking goals and teaching strategies into their regular courses.

Freshman-year experiences

A step beyond the single introductory course or pair of courses is an integrative approach to the freshman year. In some cases, this approach is the extent of the program; in others, the freshman year provides a bridge to a curriculumwide program to develop and refine students' reasoning abilities in many contexts.

The ADAPT program, offered as an option to freshmen at the University of Nebraska–Lincoln since the early 1970s, for example, helps students develop formal thinking as defined by Piaget. Faculty who teach introductory courses in several disciplines agree to organize their sections around a common core of reasoning skills—for example, observing, recording, classifying, comparing, and contrasting—and critical tests. Originally, each skill was emphasized during the same period in all courses in the program so that participating students could practice using the same skill in multiple contexts (Fuller 1978), but this practice seems to have been abandoned. The primary pedagogical method, however, remains the "learning cycle," an inductive, hands-on approach based on Piaget's theory of cognitive development. Evaluations during the first three years of the program indicated a positive influence on students' formal reasoning abilities as well as critical thinking skills (see Fuller 1980 for details).

In the intervening years, many institutions have developed programs based on Piagetian concepts. Integration of Piagetian strategies with more recent developments in cognitive psychology is exemplified in the SOAR program at Xavier University (Carmichael 1982). SOAR offers preparation for college courses, especially in science, in special summer sessions for entering freshmen at this historically black college. Results have been positive in terms of students' persistence in college and admission to medical schools. These programs have typically been implemented outside the regular curriculum.

Reasoning that the bureaucratic nature of university settings distorts the conditions for critical thinking, a professor of sociology designed a program to create a distinct "freshman learning community" within the University of Wisconsin–Oshkosh (Stark 1987). In this residential program, four groups of 30 students take clusters of three general education courses offered by faculty specially selected for the program. The courses are organized around a theme, "Tradition and the Modern World"; participating faculty work together to develop integrative, innovative approaches to their courses. Released time allows faculty to collaborate with each other and to interact informally with students outside the classroom. The evaluation will address both qualitative and quantitative aspects of the program, which is funded by the Fund for Improvement of Post-Secondary Education (FIPSE).

Freshman-year programs can stand alone, as the above descriptions suggest, or they may serve as a bridge to a curriculum that self-consciously attempts to develop critical thinking and other abilities valued in college graduates. The freshman "core curriculum" at King's College exemplifies the bridge approach. Faculty at King's College view the "curriculum as a plan of learning rather than as a mere collection of courses" (Farmer 1988, p. 61). Eight transferable skills of liberal learning, including critical thinking, define the core curriculum. Several core courses to teach these skills have been designed by faculty teams, which also monitor implementation of the courses. Faculty in every discipline have developed "competence growth plans" that link core skills with disciplinary learning and specify how those skills will be further developed in advanced courses in the major. The critical thinking course is already in place. In a recent survey of faculty, the critical thinking team found that faculty want the course to emphasize argument skills, writing argumentative essays, and sensitivity to disciplinary differences in critical thinking.

In addition to serving as a bridge to future courses, freshman-year experiences can help freshmen integrate their current learning. This principle is exemplified by Alverno College's curriculum for the freshman year. All general education courses introduce students to the critical thinking skills of analysis and communication. This instruction is supplemented by required "integrative seminars" designed to motivate involvement in learning, stimulate reflection on learning, and teach students how to integrate their learning. In the seminars, students analyze their learning needs and career possibilities to set the stage for college work. Students learn a strategy for analyzing the frameworks found in readings for their other courses. Structured journal assignments teach basic skills and terminology of analysis, such as observation and generalization. Students also learn group problem-solving skills (Loacker et al. 1984).

"Thinking across the curriculum"
Integrated instruction in critical thinking at the curricular level remains a rare phenomenon. Several small colleges, however, have achieved a relatively high degree of curricular coherence by focusing on the development of students' thinking skills.

Within larger institutions, special programs provide opportunities for the development of cross-curricular thinking skills.

At King's College, departments identify selected courses in the major to incorporate objectives of critical thinking. Growth plans developed by faculty specify required courses at the freshman through senior levels and state specific objectives for critical thinking that will be addressed in them. Feedback from course-embedded assessment and diagnostic projects keeps students aware of their progress. (See Appendix A in Farmer 1988 for a sample growth plan for students in marketing.)

Similarly, at Alverno College, course-embedded assessment of sequenced analytical abilities fosters curricular coherence and helps students learn to use critical thinking abilities in many situations. For analysis and communication as well as the other abilities emphasized at Alverno, faculty have identified levels of achievement and criteria for evaluating students' performance at each level. Rather than viewing critical thinking as a "generic" ability, Alverno faculty teach students to become aware of the context out of which their thinking arises and to use contextual information like political or social forces to understand particular problems or phenomena. The curriculum also helps students understand and reason within multiple frameworks, modes of communication, and learning methodologies. Finally, the curriculum individualizes learning by helping students learn to assess their own learning and performance and to build upon it (Loacker et al. 1984).

In the King's College and Alverno College programs, assessment is a central aspect of the learning process. In each case, however, global, "discipline-neutral" assessments are rejected in favor of assessments embedded in the learning process and tied to students' developing knowledge base. Methods such as portfolio evaluation (Belanoff and Elbow 1986) give faculty an overview of the quality of students' work while providing students with feedback on their progress. (See Farmer 1988 for a brief description of portfolio evaluation in finance.) Standardized "generic" measures may not reflect the influence of specific educational experiences on students' intellectual growth (Mentkowski and Rogers 1985).

At St. Joseph's College (Indiana), thinking and communication are also integral parts of an unusual core curriculum that extends over four years. Core courses challenge students to confront diversity, to contrast alternative world views such as

those of science and religion, to integrate their learning, and to question accepted views. Sixty percent of the faculty teach in the core program; they lecture on topics in their disciplines but often lead discussions in areas where they have less background (Gamson and Associates 1984). In contrast to King's College and Alverno, assessment is not a major theme in the program; rather, the emphasis is on interdisciplinary dialogue among students and faculty, with faculty learning and growth as much a part of the community as that of students. Students claim the program has taught them to "think and define problems better," to be "more inquisitive," to examine their values, to look at alternatives, and to be more compassionate (pp. 38–39). One student said specifically, "Core has taught me that there are no easy solutions to most problems." Faculty, too, report growth. For example, one faculty member, commenting on teaching in a cross-disciplinary context, told evaluators, "Fifteen years ago I was king of the mountain. Now I have to listen to my colleagues" (p. 36).

At SUNY–Stony Brook, an integrative approach capitalizes on the rich environment of a university while providing the benefits of a cross-curricular model and sidestepping the problems of curricular reform in university settings. "Federated learning communities" (FLCs) are the vehicle for this strategy, which takes the existing curriculum as given. FLCs are structured around three to fifteen courses over a period of one to three semesters. Themes unify this collection of existing courses, and students in the community "travel as a subgroup through the courses, which also include students not enrolled in the full FLC program" (Gamson and Associates 1984, p. 85). Faculty who teach the courses meet weekly for planning and discussion. One additional faculty member, designated a "master learner," and one graduate student take the courses and teach an integrative seminar; all participating faculty team teach a monthly core course intended to "integrate and apply" course content. Students gradually take over responsibility for the course. Students may continue their involvement with the theme of the FLC by registering for an interdisciplinary project guided by two participating faculty members (Gamson and Associates 1984).

At SUNY–Fredonia, the General College Program has replaced the earlier first-year program, the General Liberal Education Program. The new program is structured in three developmentally sequenced tiers rather than along disciplinary lines. In the first tier, students complete courses that emphasize skill areas identified as central by faculty; reasoning is an integral part of all these courses. The second tier includes introductory disciplinary courses. To be included in the program, a course must include writing and reasoning requirements and attention to implications for other fields. In the third tier, interdisciplinary or cross-cultural courses emphasize reasoning, writing, and values; students must complete term papers that demonstrate critical, integrative, and independent thinking. Faculty at the college are developing their own measures of students' growth in a major FIPSE-funded project currently in progress (Amiran 1986).

Many other strategies for teaching "thinking across the curriculum" are possible. The few presented here indicate the diverse possibilities that exist, even within the confines of relatively traditional academic institutions. How do such programs come into being? Strategies for organizational change are discussed in the following section.

Organizational Strategies

Strategies for organizational change can be formal and voluntary or moderately formal and "strongly encouraged." Informal organizational strategies may help to establish a climate for innovation, but major curricular change is unlikely to occur without formal structures and leadership bolstered by administrative support.

Informal strategies

Informal strategies depend on faculty interest and initiative. They include voluntary professional development seminars, consortia, and networks. Seminars may take the form of extended study groups, often with an emphasis on developing and testing applications of critical thinking in specific disciplinary courses (Meyers 1986; Michalak 1986). Many programs employ faculty development seminars, both to stimulate and to supplement more formal curriculum development projects (Amiran 1986; Farmer 1988).

Like seminars, regional consortia provide opportunities for faculty to learn relevant concepts and offer peer support for implementation. The East Central College Consortium Critical Thinking Project, directed by Larry Grimes of Bethany College and funded by FIPSE, uses William Perry's theory of development to help faculty understand students' reasoning and to help them consider how their teaching might foster intellectual growth. In a three-college consortium project, faculty met to study material on critical thinking, then planned courses based on what they learned, and reconvened after the courses were taught to discuss what they had found (Michalak 1986). The Minnesota Community College System supports a systemwide Writing Across the Curriculum program that has recently begun to investigate the use of writing to promote development of students' critical thinking and intellectual abilities. Another state-level initiative is the Task Force on Thinking Skills in New Jersey, which recently produced a report (Daly 1986) and is working with the Educational Testing Service to develop definitions and assessments in many disciplines. Finally, Alverno College developed a series of discipline-based networks to study critical thinking in science, arts and humanities, psychology, and management. Network members from across the country met in the summer to define critical thinking and develop strategies for teaching and assessing it in the disciplines. The network concept, which was funded by FIPSE, has produced two books to date (Cromwell 1986; Halonen 1986).

Formal institutionally sponsored strategies

Formal strategies generally focus on curriculum development. Campus leaders organize faculty committees or teams to study critical thinking skills specifically, or the teams may be assigned to identify needed changes in general education programs or develop curricular goals and assessment strategies, out of which a concern with critical thinking skills frequently emerges.

Drawing on its experience with a formal planning model (Bergquist and Armstrong 1986), King's College has made extensive use of faculty "project teams" that not only study and make recommendations but also implement, monitor, and support curricular changes. Faculty attend conferences in teams so that innovators will have a support group on campus. Teams create course syllabi together, first identifying learning outcomes, then specifying assignments, examinations, and appropriate pedagogy. Its initiator describes the change process as "organic." "General goals have been set forth for the design and implementation of an outcomes-oriented curriculum supported by a course-embedded assessment model." Within this broad, flexible framework, faculty have initiated "virtually a hundred experiments," with varying degrees of success but an overall spirit of cooperation and colleagueship (Farmer 1988, p. 160).

A program called "Development of Thinking Skills," or DOTS, is the product of a five-phase curriculum development process used by faculty at Kapiolani Community College in Hawaii. In phase 1, Exploration and Assessment, the "essential task" was to study concepts of thinking and approaches to teaching thinking. Phase 2, Focusing and Setting Directions, posed the question, "Given the possibilities, what can KCC do to help its students develop and refine their thinking skills?" A steering committee developed a comprehensive three-year institutional plan and definitions of key terms, such as "critical thinking" and "cognitive operations." The goals included providing information and activities on thinking skills for students and faculty, assessing students' performance and disseminating the data for "collegewide discussions, suggestions, and actions" (p. 16), and evaluating the project to learn what activities foster student and faculty development.

In phase 3, Organize and Prepare, the committee sought faculty input and observations about students' needs in thinking skills, set up project management and priorities, developed demonstration activities in several courses, and tested an assessment instrument. In phase 4, Implement and Observe, the project was formally initiated for a three-year period. Evaluation of the first project year revealed that sharing project information stimulated wider participation by faculty and that participation and acceptance resulted from its emphasis on discipline-specific teaching goals and careful use of research in all project phases. "Open institutional support for this process makes it easier for faculty to take risks, try the new and different, and be creative" (Lanzilotti n.d., p. 17).

Institutional assessment of learning outcomes has recently received attention as a way to stimulate curricular and instructional reform generally and may have some usefulness for critical thinking outcomes. Assessment of baccalaureate outcomes, including critical thinking skills, was the focus of a major project supported by the American Association of State Colleges and Universities (1986). Participating colleges used a systematic model to define desired outcomes and develop assessments. Participants sometimes found themselves confronted by an unexpected challenge, however: "Much controversy and more than a little impatience were evident as we discovered we often differed widely on what students should know and be able to do. Perhaps more frustrating, we found ourselves in frequent disagreement about pedagogical values, styles, and philosophies. Faculty members perhaps assume too much about campus consistency on such issues when not faced directly with empirical evidence of diversity" (AASCU 1986, p. 41).

Contentiousness can arise if faculty are uncertain how institutional-level assessment data will be used. Assessment should be clearly distinguished from program evaluation, but often the two terms are used interchangeably. Assessment implies "*sitting down beside or together* (from late Latin *ad* + *sedere*) to render an "expert judgment . . . on the basis of careful observation" (Loacker, Cromwell, and O'Brien 1986, p. 47). It is descriptive rather than quantitative; its purpose is to help individual learners improve upon and internalize criteria for judging their own performance. In contrast, evaluation aims to make conclusions about groups of students to render judgment on programs (Loacker, Cromwell, and O'Brien 1986). Assessment is most useful to students when it is embedded within courses and is primarily intended to help them monitor their progress. This philosophy is evident at both King's College and Alverno. (For further discussions of assessment, see Jacobi, Astin, and Ayala 1987 and McMillan 1988.)

Faculty may accept assessment of critical thinking most readily if it supports an innovative program that is already under way. For example, among AASCU's projects, Chico State University reported success in part because program revisions in general education had already been initiated by faculty. Similarly, at SUNY–Fredonia, faculty are actively involved in developing and validating their own assessments for the eight core skills in their General College Program.

Proponents of institutional-level assessment report that even "generic" assessments have had noteworthy effects on teaching practices relevant to critical thinking. Specifically, feedback from assessment programs in Tennessee colleges and universities has prompted faculty to be more explicit about course objectives, to align instruction and testing more closely with stated objectives, to increase writing assignments, to demand more higher-order thinking skills in their courses, and to provide more opportunities for students to apply knowledge through active learning methods (Banta and Fisher 1986).

Features of Current Programs

Institutional programs to develop students' critical thinking skills share a number of features, although they are not uniform in their history, structure, or methods. A few are suggested here; more experience with such programs is needed to identify necessary and sufficient conditions of innovation aimed at students' intellectual growth.

1. Faculty ownership and voluntary participation in equilibrium with administrative support and direction. Time for planning and faculty collaboration are provided by a supportive administration or external grant. Faculty and institutional development are intertwined with a common focus on development of curriculum for students' growth.
2. Small college setting *or* special program within a large university. Facilities for informal, out-of-class conversation are desirable, especially for programs at commuter colleges (Gamson and Associates 1984).
3. Focus on critical thinking outcomes within a broad operational framework adaptable to disciplinary variations.
4. Assessment used for feedback to students rather than for program evaluation. Consequently, assessment is embedded in disciplinary courses, assessments are locally developed to reflect the curriculum, assessments are qualitative as well as quantitative, incorporating oral and written student performance and products, criteria are publicly stated and known to students, and multiple occasions for assessment keep students informed of their growth.
5. Alignment of goals, methods, and evaluation procedures. Thus, goals of instruction are explicitly stated within a broad framework, instructional methods are active and participatory so students can practice reasoning skills specified in the curriculum, and evaluation more closely reflects what is to be learned.
6. Interdisciplinary discussion of the aims and methods of education in both formal and informal programs.

Consequences for Academic Life

Participants and leaders of the programs described here emphasize colleagueship and consciously seek to foster community. Students expressly acknowledge the community they experience in these programs. Building intellectual communities "does not take a lot of money or a residential institution . . . . Rather, attention to how the curriculum is structured to affect social relationships is critical" (Gamson and Associates 1984, p. 90; see also Stark 1987). A student in one of Stony Brook's federated learning communities says, "I have come to appreciate the importance of academic discussion with my fellow students. I spend much more time discussing what I learn in schools with my friends" (Gamson and Associates 1984, p. 86). Faculty, too, emphasize the intellectually stimulating and motivating aspects of cooperative inquiry.

What are the effects of these programs on students' abilities to think critically? Too few programs have been implemented to draw a firm conclusion. Students' own reports and reports from faculty observers, however, suggest that program "graduates" are more aggressive learners than the "passive" students faculty often describe. They question. They inquire. They refuse to "take things at face value" (Gamson and Associates 1984, p. 90). These observations support the hope that broad-based, collaboratively developed programs can help students develop both abilities and dispositions of critical thinkers.

CONCLUSION

The model of education for critical thinking suggested in this report emphasizes curriculumwide integration of content and reasoning. There are no shortcuts: Participating in sustained, guided, collaborative inquiry is the only way to learn its methods, its epistemology, and its value. Excessive emphasis on "efficient" transmission of large quantities of information is costly in the long run, because it crowds out time students need to transform information into meaningful, usable knowledge. Students will respond to instruction that invites them to use knowledge to make sense of important human questions.

All of which is not to say that every course must become a forum for debating global issues or questions of personal identity. It does suggest, however, that educators must help students discover *purpose* in learning. A problem or question that arouses students' sense of wonder can provoke the desire to understand a subject more fully and provide the motivation for sustained inquiry (Meyers 1986). Moreover, critical thinking need not, and probably should not, be an isolated, individual activity. Motivation to think deeply thrives in a supportive community of peers, guided by a teacher who is willing to step off stage a good deal of the time to let students figure things out for themselves (Finkel and Monk 1978, 1983).

Teaching for critical thinking does not take place in a vacuum. Students frequently bring with them both a home culture and a peer culture with norms that may be antithetical to critical questioning. Uncritical thinking, either as dualism/received knowledge or as multiplicity/subjective knowledge, is a pervasive and resilient counterforce that does not evaporate when students enter the classroom.

Throughout this report, the reader has found examples of teachers and researchers who have fostered critical thinking with diverse students and in diverse educational settings. Their efforts provide inspiration and direction for future research and practice.

A high priority is research on the effectiveness of preparatory courses in critical thinking skills.

Needed Research

Teaching thinking, especially in the disciplines, is a field wide open for research. Research is needed on the effectiveness of general introductory courses in critical thinking skills, on relationships between knowledge and reasoning abilities, and on instructional and institutional conditions that nurture critical inquiry. Individual differences in approaches to critical thinking merit exploration, particularly those related to gender, ethnicity, and learning style. Studies of critical thinking and behavior offer a promising area for research.

A high priority is research on the effectiveness of preparatory courses in critical thinking skills. Currently, evidence of their effectiveness is primarily anecdotal. Research is needed to assess the effects of various approaches on reading skills and reasoning abilities (including construction as well as analysis of arguments) and on performance in subsequent courses. Research is also needed on relationships between knowledge and reasoning abilities and on instructional and institutional conditions that nurture critical inquiry.

Teacher-initiated classroom studies offer inquisitive instructors a means to explore their questions about learning in their classrooms. Questions might range from "What do students already know, or think they know, about this subject when they start the course?" to "What happens to class dynamics when I introduce value-laden questions early in the term as opposed to late?" Answering such questions does not require elaborate instrumentation. The primary requisite is a reasonably well-formulated question and a strategy for gathering information about it (see Cross and Angelo 1988 for examples). Such studies can present unexpected challenges and inevitably raise new questions, however (Erickson and Erickson 1988).

Naturalistic studies of students at work on actual class assignments, using the "think-aloud" method or working in pairs, would provide a much-needed balance to the artificiality of many laboratory studies on problem solving, particularly if students were observed over a period of weeks as their investigations progressed. Extended observation would clarify the mutual influences of reading, writing, and discussion in completing actual critical thinking projects.

Many questions suggest themselves with respect to the role of knowledge, cognition, and metacognition in critical thinking. Analysis of the nature and structure of knowledge in the disciplines and research on how this knowledge is acquired and used has only begun to scratch the surface of this important field of inquiry. Much needed are discipline-based studies of the role of knowledge in thinking and of methods of instruction that increase understanding, organization, and accessibility of knowledge for critical thinking. Few studies examine methods for teaching discipline-specific strategic knowledge, yet it is precisely this knowledge that theoretically must be made more explicit in teaching. Collaborations between disciplinary experts and cognitive researchers afford both a fresh and stimulating view of their subjects.

Questions remain about metacognition, for example, its transferability and the extent to which it can increase access to knowledge. Many composition textbooks include rhetorical "invention" strategies to help students generate ideas for essays. They function as metacognitive prompts; their persistence since Aristotle compiled them suggests that they are a valuable resource in thinking. Strategies for analyzing characteristics of audiences and anticipating objections may also serve a metacognitive function. They impose constraints that may help or hinder development of arguments, depending on what stage of the process they are introduced. The role of such devices in accessing knowledge and promoting objectivity merits study.

Peers are now recognized as a valuable resource in learning. Questions of how to organize classes for peer collaboration persist among teachers; classroom studies are needed at the college level. Important research is needed to pursue Vygotsky's hypothesis (1978) that students "internalize" reasoning processes gleaned from collaborations with peers.

Research is needed to reveal how the *disposition* to think critically arises. Studies of student-faculty interactions have already demonstrated a significant role of faculty in students' academic commitment (Pascarella 1980). Closer analysis of such interactions could reveal factors that encourage critical thinking, for example, the teacher's role as a model for students. More studies of relationships between knowledge, beliefs about knowledge, and learning strategies might provide a better understanding of how this disposition develops. For example, what kinds of discipline-related questions are most likely to arouse students' curiosity? What misconceptions do students commonly share, and how can they be dislodged? The role of affect in critical thinking merits much greater attention (McLeod 1985).

The "culture" of a classroom can also be studied to understand how participants give meaning to their interactions and how those meanings shape the learning situation (Bolster 1983). Cultural studies would help to unravel the complex interactions that arise when students experience unaccustomed expectations for independent or collaborative inquiry.

The context for critical thinking, too, must be examined more fully. Undergraduates' minimal devotion to studies and the infrequency of library use have been documented (Boyer

1987). What factors in students' environment foster these behaviors? How can they be counteracted? How can the cocurriculum of the institution be designed to encourage mature "habits of the mind" among students?

Expert practice in teaching is also an important subject of study for understanding how critical thinking can be taught. Much can be learned by identifying teachers who successfully emphasize thinking skills, talking with them, studying their planning processes, observing their classes, talking with their students, and reviewing their students' work.

Support and Dissemination
Institutional support for instruction in critical thinking in the disciplines entails sensitivity to the kind of classroom environment in which teaching takes place. Class size is a consideration, for although large classes can be adapted to allow critical thinking, faculty who tackle this challenge often put in long hours grading papers and talking with students. When large classes are unavoidable, teaching assistants and/or graders are a wise institutional investment. Advanced undergraduates can often fill these roles. Training and supervision of teaching assistants is essential, regardless of their educational level. Large classes that do not have discussion sections can employ small groups to personalize the learning environment (Michaelsen 1983; Monk 1983). Professors who emphasize thinking should be acknowledged and supported in the promotion and tenure review process.

Nationally, faculty can share information about teaching in general, and critical thinking in particular, in both disciplinary and interdisciplinary forums. Administrators who want to see more instruction in critical thinking on their campuses can set aside funds to send a team of faculty to one or more conferences. They may also want to establish a fund to support classroom and laboratory studies on teaching thinking.

Many disciplinary associations have divisions and journals devoted to education. In some cases, however, little attention is paid to development of thinking skills in the discipline. More professional activism in this direction is needed to increase the legitimacy of teaching research and provide outlets for the exchange of ideas and experimental work on instruction (Mauksch and Howery 1986).

A worthwhile project for disciplinary associations to undertake is the close scrutiny of textbooks in their fields used in public schools. Textbooks provide the background knowledge students bring with them to college; many are dull, poorly written, too abstract or too simplistic, and misleading (see Kahane 1984 for examples). Associations might support model projects for cooperative evaluation of textbooks in local and regional schools, or they might establish national projects to attract attention to the problem of poor texts.

Institutions are situated within communities, and educators cannot afford to ignore the social context in which attempts to foster critical thinking are embedded. The popular media do not favor extended discussion of significant questions (Postman 1985a, 1985b). Educational institutions, by the example they set in their programs, can exacerbate or counteract this tendency. When educational institutions sponsor public programs with a single authoritative speaker, they reinforce simplistic concepts of knowledge. Programs that feature several speakers, each with a different point of view, embody a more pluralistic epistemology. The educational value of such programs is enhanced if both speakers and audience exchange ideas, perhaps guided by ground rules to ensure thoughtful discussion.

There is no shortage of work to be done in this arena. The path is a long one, surrounded by thickets, but it is wide enough to accommodate a diverse community of travelers. All educators can contribute to understanding and promoting critical thinking, simply by turning in the direction of their own teaching and learning and recognizing the challenges their students face. A journey of this kind has no end. But it promises deeper understanding of one's discipline and greater appreciation of its meaning for students and for society. Along the way are the many satisfactions of helping students discover the motivating force of intellectual purpose.

REFERENCES

The Educational Resources Information Center (ERIC) Clearinghouse
on Higher Education abstracts and indexes the current literature on
higher education for inclusion in ERIC's data base and announcement
in ERIC's monthly bibliographic journal, *Resources in Education*
(RIE). Most of these publications are available through the ERIC
Document Reproduction Service (EDRS). For publications cited in this
bibliography that are available from EDRS, ordering number and price
are included. Readers who wish to order a publication should write to
the ERIC Document Reproduction Service, 3900 Wheeler Avenue,
Alexandria, Virginia 22304. (Phone orders with VISA or MasterCard are
taken at 800/227-ERIC or 703/823-0500.) When ordering, please specify
the document (ED or HE) number. Documents are available as noted in
microfiche (MF) and paper copy (PC). Because prices are subject to
change, it is advisable to check the latest issue of *Resources in Education* for
current cost based on the number of pages in the publication.

Alvermann, Donna E., D.R. Dillon, and D.G. O'Brien. 1987. *Using
Discussion to Promote Reading Comprehension*. Newark, Del.: International Reading Association.

American Association of State Colleges and Universities. 1986. *Defining and Assessing Baccalaureate Skills: A Report on the Academic
Program Evaluation Project*. Washington, D.C.: Author. ED 293
379. 81 pp. MF–$1.07; PC not available EDRS.

Amiran, Minda Rae. May 1986. "Improving Undergraduate Education: The Development of Collegewide Measures of Progress toward
Goals of General Education." Proposal to the Fund for the Improvement of Post-Secondary Education. SUNY–Fredonia. ED 280
331. 13 pp. MF–$1.07; PC–$3.85.

Anderson, John R. 1985. *Cognitive Psychology and Its Implications*.
2d ed. New York: W.H. Freeman.

Argyris, Chris, Robert Putnam, and Diana McLain Smith. 1985. *Action Science: Concepts, Methods, and Skills for Research and Intervention*. San Francisco: Jossey-Bass.

Armbruster, Bonnie B. 1984. "The Problem of 'Inconsiderate
Text.' " In *Comprehension Instruction*, edited by G. Duffy, L.
Roehler, and J. Mason. New York: Longman.

Arons, Arnold. 1976. "Cultivating the Capacity for Formal Reasoning:
Objectives and Procedures in an Introductory Physical Science
Course." *American Journal of Physics* 44(9): 834–38.

———. Summer 1985. " 'Critical Thinking' and the Baccalaureate
Curriculum." *Liberal Education* 71: 141–57.

Banta, Trudy, and Homer S. Fisher. 1986. "Assessing Outcomes: The
Real Value Added Is in the Process." In *Legislative Action and As-
sessment: Reason and Reality*, compiled by Kathleen McGuinness.
Proceedings from the Conference on Legislative Action and Assess-
ment: Reason and Reality. George Mason University and AASCU,
Arlington, Virginia.

Barnes, Carol P. 1983. "Questioning in College Classrooms." In *Studies of College Teaching*, edited by Carolyn L. Ellner and Carol P. Barnes. Lexington, Mass.: Lexington Books.

Barry, Vincent. 1983. *Good Reason for Writing*. Belmont, Cal.: Wadsworth.

Bartlett, F.C. 1932. *Remembering: An Experimental and Social Study*. New York: Cambridge Univ. Press.

Baxter-Magolda, Marcia. 1987. "The Affective Dimension of Learning: Faculty-Student Relationships that Enhance Intellectual Development." Miami Univ. (Ohio).

Baxter-Magolda, Marcia, and William D. Porterfield. 1985. "A New Approach to Assess Intellectual Development on the Perry Scheme." *Journal of College Student Personnel* 26(4): 343–51.

Bean, John C., and John D. Ramage. 1986. *Form and Surprise in Composition: Writing and Thinking across the Curriculum*. New York: Macmillan.

Beardsley, Monroe C. 1975. *Thinking Straight: Principles of Reasoning for Readers and Writers*. 4th ed. Englewood Cliffs, N.J.: Prentice-Hall.

Belanoff, Pat, and Peter Elbow. 1986. "Using Portfolios to Increase Collaboration and Community in a Writing Program." *Writing Program Administrator* 9(3): 27–39.

Belenky, Mary F., Blythe M. Clinchy, Nancy R. Goldberger, and Jill M. Tarule. 1985. "Epistemological Development and the Politics of Talk in Family Life." *Journal of Education* 167(3): 9–27.

———. 1986. *Women's Ways of Knowing: The Development of Self, Voice, and Mind*. New York: Basic Books.

Benack, Suzanne. 1982. "The Coding of Dimensions of Epistemological Thought in Young Men and Women." *Moral Education Forum* 7(2): 3–23.

———. 1984. "Postformal Epistemologies and the Growth of Empathy." In *Beyond Formal Operations: Late Adolescent and Adult Cognitive Development*, edited by M.L. Commons, F. Richards, and C. Armon. New York: Praeger.

Benack, Suzanne, and Michael Basseches. 1987. "Dialectical Thinking and Relativistic Epistemology." In *Advances in the Study of Adult Cognition*. New York: Praeger.

Benware, Carl A., and Edward L. Deci. 1984. "Quality of Learning with an Active versus Passive Motivational Set." *American Educational Research Journal* 21(4): 775–65.

Bergquist, Wm. H., and Jack L. Armstrong. 1986. *Planning Effectively for Educational Quality*. San Francisco: Jossey-Bass.

Bernstein, David. 1988. "When Inquiry Goes Wrong: Some Biases in Students' Reasoning and Their Use of Evidence." Paper presented at the Symposium on the Role of Inquiry and the Scientific Method, University of Sarajevo and Grand Valley State University, April.

Bernstein, David A., and Rosanne Brouwer. 1986. "Evaluating a Critical Thinking Course in Psychology." Proceedings of the 5th National Conference on Intellectual Skills Development, November, Kalamazoo, Michigan.

Berthoff, Anne E. 1984. "Is Teaching Still Possible? Writing, Meaning, and Higher-Order Reasoning." *College English* 46: 743–55.

Bizell, Patricia. September 1984. "William Perry and Liberal Education." *College English* 46: 447–54.

———. 1986. "What Happens When Basic Writers Come to College?" *College Composition and Communication* 37(3): 294–301.

Bloom, Allan. 1987. *The Closing of the American Mind: How Higher Education Has Failed Democracy and Impoverished the Souls of Today's Students*. New York: Simon & Schuster.

Bloom, Benjamin S., and Lois J. Broder. 1950. *Problem-Solving Processes of College Students: An Exploratory Investigation*. Supplementary Educational Monographs No. 73. Chicago: Univ. of Chicago Press.

Bolster, Arthur S. 1983. "Toward a More Effective Model of Research on Teaching." *Harvard Educational Review* 53(3): 294–308.

Boyer, Ernest L. 1987. *College: The Undergraduate Experience in America*. New York: Harper & Row.

Boylan, Michael. 1988. *The Process of Argument*. Englewood Cliffs, N.J.: Prentice-Hall.

Brabeck, Mary. 1983. "Critical Thinking Skills and Reflective Judgment Development: Redefining the Aims of Higher Education." *Journal of Applied Developmental Psychology* 4: 23–34.

Bransford, J., R. Sherwood, N. Vye, and J. Rieser. 1986. "Teaching Thinking and Problem Solving: Research Foundations." *American Psychologist* 41(10): 1078–89.

Brookfield, Stephen D. 1987. *Developing Critical Thinkers: Challenging Adults to Explore Alternative Ways of Thinking and Acting*. San Francisco: Jossey-Bass.

Broughton, John M. 1975. "The Development of Natural Epistemology in Adolescence and Early Adulthood." Ph.D. dissertation, Harvard Univ.

Browne, M.N., and S.M. Keeley. 1986. *Asking the Right Questions: A Guide to Critical Thinking*. 2d ed. Englewood Cliffs, N.J.: Prentice-Hall.

Carey, Susan. 1986. "Cognitive Science and Science Education." *American Psychologist* 41(10): 1123–30.

Carmichael, J.W., Jr. 1982. "Improving Problem-Solving Skills: Minority Students and the Health Professions." In *Summer Programs for Underprepared Freshmen*, edited by K.V. Lauridsen and C.F. Myers. New Directions in College Learning Assistance No. 10. San Francisco: Jossey-Bass.

Carmichael, J.W., Johnette Hassell, Jacqueline T. Hunter, Lester Jones, Mary Ann Ryan, and Harold Vincent. 1980. "Project SOAR (Stress on Analytical Reasoning)." *American Biology Teacher* 42(3): 169–73.

Carpenter, C. Blaine, and James C. Doig. 1988. "Assessing Critical Thinking across the Curriculum." In *Assessing Students' Learning*, edited by James H. McMillan. New Directions for Teaching and Learning No. 34. San Francisco: Jossey-Bass.

Carpenter, Elizabeth T. 1980. "Piagetian Interviews of College Students." In *Piagetian Programs in Higher Education*, edited by Robert G. Fuller. Lincoln: Univ. of Nebraska–Lincoln.

Cerbin, B. 1988. "The Nature and Development of Informal Reasoning Skills in College Students." Paper presented at the 12th National Institute on Issues in Teaching and Learning, "Teaching Critical Thinking: Campus Practice, Emerging Connections," April 24–27, Chicago, Illinois. HE 021 666. 17 pp. MF–$1.07; PC–$3.85.

Chase, W.G., and Herbert A. Simon. 1973. "The Mind's Eye in Chess." In *Visual Information Processing*, edited by W.G. Chase. New York: Academic Press.

Chi, Michelene T.H., Paul J. Feltovich, and Robert Glaser. 1981. "Categorization and Representation of Physics Problems by Experts and Novices." *Cognitive Science* 5: 121–52.

Chickering, Arthur. 1969. *Education and Identity*. San Francisco: Jossey-Bass.

———. 1974. *Commuting vs. Resident Students: Overcoming the Inequities of Living Off Campus*. San Francisco: Jossey-Bass.

Christensen, C. Roland. 1987. *Teaching with the Case Method: Text, Cases, and Reading*. Boston: Harvard Business School.

Claxton, Charles S., and Patricia Murrell. 1987. *Learning Styles: Implications for Educational Practices*. ASHE-ERIC Higher Education Report No. 4. Washington, D.C.: Association for the Study of Higher Education. HE 021 434. 106 pp. MF–$1.07; PC–$12.07.

Claxton, Charles S., and Yvonne Ralston. 1978. *Learning Styles: Their Impact on Teaching and Administration*. AAHE-ERIC Higher Education Report No. 10. Washington, D.C.: American Association for Higher Education. ED 167 065. 74 pp. MF–$1.07; PC–$7.73.

Clement, J. 1983. "A Conceptual Model Discussed by Galileo and Used Intuitively by Physics Students." In *Mental Models*, edited by Dedre Gentner and Albert L. Stevens. Hillsdale, N.J.: Erlbaum Associates.

Clinchy, Blythe, Judy Lief, and Pamela Young. 1977. "Epistemological and Moral Development in Girls from a Traditional and a Progressive High School." *Journal of Educational Psychology* 69(4): 337–43.

Clinchy, Blythe, and Claire Zimmerman. 1982. "Epistemology and Agency in the Development of Undergraduate Women." In *The*

Undergraduate Woman: Issues in Educational Equity, edited by Pamela J. Perun. Lexington, Mass.: Lexington Books.

Cohen, Elizabeth. 1986. *Designing Groupwork: Strategies for the Heterogeneous Classroom*. New York: Teachers College Press.

Collins, Allan, John S. Brown, and Susan E. Newman. 1986. "Cognitive Apprenticeship: Teaching the Craft of Reading, Writing, and Mathematics." In *Cognition and Instruction: Issues and Agendas*, edited by Lauren B. Resnick. Hillsdale, N.J.: Erlbaum Associates.

Collins, Allan, and Albert L. Stevens. 1982. "Goals and Strategies of Inquiry Teachers." In *Advances in Instructional Psychology*, vol. 2, edited by Robert Glaser. Hillsdale, N.J.: Erlbaum Associates.

Collins, Michael J., ed. 1983. *Teaching Values and Ethics in College*. New Directions for Teaching and Learning No. 13. San Francisco: Jossey-Bass.

Copi, Irving M. 1986. *Informal Logic*. New York: Macmillan.

Coward, Pat, and Jo Taylor. 1983. "Composition and Science: A Symbiotic Relationship." Paper presented at the meeting of the Midwest Writing Centers Conference, October, Iowa City, Iowa. ED 238 001. 12 pp. MF–$1.07; PC–$3.85.

Cromwell, Lucy, ed. 1986. *Teaching Critical Thinking in the Arts and Humanities*. Milwaukee: Alverno Productions.

Cross, K. Patricia, and Thomas A. Angelo. 1988. *Classroom Assessment Techniques: A Handbook for Faculty*. Technical Report No. 88-A-004.0. Ann Arbor: Univ. of Michigan, NCRIPTAL.

Cuban, Larry. 1984. "Policy and Research Dilemmas in the Teaching of Reasoning: Unplanned Designs." *Review of Educational Research* 54(4): 655–81.

Daly, William T. March 1986. *Thinking Skills: An Overview*. Trenton: New Jersey Basic Skills Council, Dept. of Higher Education. ED 272 442. 68 pp. MF–$1.07; PC–$7.73.

Dewey, John. 1933. *How We Think*. Chicago: Henry Regnery.

———. 1938. *Experience and Education*. New York: Collier Books.

Dillon, J.T. 1984. "Research on Questioning and Discussion." *Educational Leadership* 42(3): 50–56.

diSessa, Andrea A. 1983. "Phenomenology and the Evolution of Intuition." In *Mental Models*, edited by Dedre Gentner and Albert L. Stevens. Hillsdale, N.J.: Erlbaum Associates.

Dressel, Paul L., and Irvin J. Lehmann. Summer 1965. "The Impact of Higher Education on Student Attitudes, Values, and Critical Thinking Abilities." *Educational Record*: 248–58.

Duncker, K. 1945. "On Problem Solving." *Psychological Monographs* 58: 1–110.

Durst, Russel K. 1987. "Cognitive and Linguistic Demands of Analytic Writing." *Research in the Teaching of English* 21(4): 347–76.

Ennis, Robert H. 1962. "A Concept of Critical Thinking." *Harvard Educational Review* 32(1): 81–111.

————. October 1985. "A Logical Basis for Measuring Critical Thinking Skills." *Educational Leadership*: 44–48.

————. 1986. "A Taxonomy of Critical Thinking Dispositions and Abilities." In *Teaching Thinking Skills*, edited by Joan B. Baron and Robert J. Sternberg. New York: W.H. Freeman.

Ennis, Robert H., and Jason Millman. 1985. *Cornell Tests of Critical Thinking*. Pacific Grove, Cal.: Midwest Publications.

Erickson, Bette, and Glenn R. Erickson. 1988. "Notes on a Classroom Research Program." In *To Improve the Academy*, vol. 7, edited by Joanne Kurfiss, Linda Hilsen, Susan Kahn, Mary Deane Sorcinelli, and Richard Tiberius. Stillwater, Okla: POD/New Forums Press.

Eylon, Bat-Sheva, and F. Reif. 1984. "Effects of Knowledge Organization on Task Performance." *Cognition and Instruction* 1(1): 5–44.

Facione, Peter A. 1984. "Toward a Theory of Critical Thinking." *Liberal Education* 70(3): 253–61.

————. 1986. "Testing College-Level Critical Thinking." *Liberal Education* 72(3): 221–31.

Faigley, Lester, and Stephen Witte. 1981. "Analyzing Revision." *College Composition and Communication* 32: 400–14.

Farmer, D.W. 1988. *Enhancing Student Learning: Emphasizing Essential Competencies in Academic Programs*. Wilkes-Barre, Pa.: King's College.

Feichtner, Susan B., and Elain A. Davis. 1984–85. "Why Some Groups Fail: A Survey of Students' Experiences with Learning Groups." *Organizational Behavior Teaching Review* 9(1): 58–73.

Finkel, Donald L., and G. Stephen Monk. 1978. "Contexts for Learning: A Teacher's Guide to the Design of Intellectual Experience." Olympia, Wash.: Evergreen State College.

————. 1983. "Teaching and Learning in Groups: Dissolution of the Atlas Complex." In *Learning in Groups*, edited by Clark Bouton and Russell Y. Garth. New Directions for Teaching and Learning No. 14. San Francisco: Jossey-Bass.

Flavell, John. 1976. "Metacognitive Aspects of Problem Solving." In *The Nature of Intelligence*, edited by Lauren Resnick. Hillsdale, N.J.: Erlbaum Associates.

————. 1979. "Metacognition and Cognitive Monitoring." *American Psychologist* 34: 906–11.

Flower, Linda, and John R. Hayes. February 1980. "The Cognition of Discovery: Defining a Rhetorical Problem." *College Composition and Communication* 31: 21–32.

Flower, Linda, John R. Hayes, Linda Carey, Karen Schriver, and James Stratman. 1986. "Detection, Diagnosis, and the Strategies of Revision." *College Composition and Communication* 37(1): 16–55.

Foos, Paul W., and Cherie M. Clark. 1983. "Learning from Text: Effects of Input Order and Expected Test." *Human Learning* 2: 177–85.

Frankenstein, Marilyn. 1987. "Critical Mathematics Education: An Application of Paulo Freire's Epistemology." In *Freire for the Classroom: A Sourcebook for Liberatory Teaching*, edited by Ira Shor. Portsmouth, N.H.: Heinemann Educational Books.

Freie, John F. 1987. "Thinking and Believing." *College Teaching* 35(3): 89–91.

Freire, Paulo. 1985. *The Politics of Education*. South Hadley, Mass.: Bergin & Garvey.

Fuller, Robert G., ed. 1978. *Multidisciplinary Piagetian-Based Programs for College Freshmen*. 3d ed. Lincoln: Univ. of Nebraska–Lincoln.

———, ed. 1980. *Piagetian Programs in Higher Education*. Lincoln: Univ. of Nebraska–Lincoln.

Furedy, John J., and Chris Furedy. 1979. "Course Design for Critical Thinking." *Improving College and University Teaching* 27(3): 99–101.

Gage, John T. 1987. *The Shape of Reason: Argumentative Writing in College*. New York: Macmillan.

Gamson, Zelda F., and Associates. 1984. *Liberating Education*. San Francisco: Jossey-Bass.

Gardner, Howard. 1985. *The Mind's New Science: A History of the Cognitive Revolution*. New York: Basic Books.

Girle, Roderic A. 1983. "A Top-Down Approach to the Teaching of Reasoning Skills." In *Thinking: The Expanding Frontier*, edited by William Maxwell. Philadelphia: Franklin Institute Press.

Glaser, Edward M. 1941. *An Experiment in the Development of Critical Thinking*. New York: Teachers College of Columbia Univ., Bureau of Publications.

Glaser, Robert. 1984. "Education and Thinking: The Role of Knowledge." *American Psychologist* 13(9): 5–10.

Goldberger, Nancy R. 1981. "Developmental Assumptions Underlying Models of General Education." *Liberal Education* 67(3): 223–43.

Greenfield, Lois Broder. 1987. "Teaching Thinking through Problem Solving." In *Developing Critical Thinking and Problem-Solving Abilities*, edited by James E. Stice. New Directions for Teaching and Learning No. 30. San Francisco: Jossey-Bass.

Greeno, James G. 1980. "Some Examples of Cognitive Task Analysis with Instructional Implications." In *Aptitude, Learning, and Instruction*, edited by R.E. Snow, P. Frederico, and W.E. Montague. Hillsdale, N.J.: Erlbaum Associates.

Guyton, Edith M. 1982. "Critical Thinking and Political Participation:

The Development and Assessment of a Causal Model." Paper presented at the annual meeting of the National Council for the Social Studies, November, Boston, Massachusetts. ED 228 116. 51 pp. MF–$1.07; PC–$7.73.

———. 1984. "An Analysis of the Cognitive Antecedents of Political Variables." Paper presented at the annual meeting of the American Educational Research Association, April, New Orleans, Louisiana. ED 245 951. 24 pp. MF–$1.07; PC–$3.85.

Halonen, Jane S. 1985. "Critical Thinking throughout the Undergraduate Psychology Curriculum." Paper presented at the Mid-America Conference for Teachers of Psychology, October, Indiana. ED 269 281. 27 pp. MF–$1.07; PC–$5.79.

———. 1986. *Teaching Critical Thinking in Psychology*. Milwaukee: Alverno Productions.

Hamblen, Karen A. 1984. "The Application of Questioning Strategy Research to Art Criticism Instruction." Paper presented at the annual meeting of the American Educational Research Association, April, New Orleans, Louisiana. ED 243 787. 30 pp. MF–$1.07; PC–$5.79.

Harding, Sandra. 1987. "Struggling for Self-Definition." *Women's Review of Books* 4(6): 6–7.

Hays, Janice N. 1987. "Models of Intellectual Development and Writing: A Response to Myra Kogen et al." *Journal of Basic Writing* 6(1): 11–27.

Hays, Janice N., Kathleen S. Brandt, and Kathryn H. Chantry. 1988. "The Impact of Friendly and Hostile Audiences upon the Argumentative Writing of High School and College Students." *Research in the Teaching of English*. In press.

Heiman, Marcia, and Joshua Slomianko. 1984. *Learning to Learn: Some Questions and Answers*. Cambridge, Mass.: Learning Skills Consultants.

Herrnstein, Richard J., Raymond S. Nickerson, Margarita de Sanchez, and John A. Swets. 1986. "Teaching Thinking Skills." *American Psychologist* 41(11): 1279–89.

Hillocks, George, Jr. November 1984. "What Works in Teaching Composition: A Meta-Analysis of Experimental Treatment Studies." *American Journal of Education* 93(1): 133–69.

———. 1986. *Research on Written Composition: New Directions for Teaching*. Urbana, Ill.: ERIC Clearinghouse on Reading and Communication Skills and National Conference on Research in English.

Hillocks, George, Jr., Elizabeth A. Kahn, and Larry R. Johannessen. 1983. "Teaching Defining Strategies as a Mode of Inquiry: Some Effects on Student Writing." *Research in the Teaching of English* 17(3): 275–84.

Hunt, D.E. 1966. "A Conceptual System Change Model and Its Application to Education." In *Experience, Structure, and Adaptability*, edited by O.J. Harvery. New York: Springer.

Hursh, Barbara A., and Lenore Borzak. 1979. "Toward Cognitive Development through Field Studies." *Journal of Higher Education* 50(1): 63–78.

Hursh, Daniel E., Claudia B. VanArsdale, Franklin J. Medio, and Rogers McAvoy. n.d. "The Effects of Guided Design on Decision-Making Skills."

Inhelder, Barbel, and Jean Piaget. 1958. *The Growth of Logical Thinking from Childhood to Adolescence*. New York: Basic Books.

Jacob, Philip E. 1957. *Changing Values in College: An Exploratory Study of the Impact of College Teaching*. New York: Harper & Row.

Jacobi, Maryann, Alexander Astin, and Frank Ayala. 1987. *College Student Outcomes Assessment: A Talent Development Perspective*. ASHE-ERIC Higher Education Report No. 7. Washington, D.C.: Association for the Study of Higher Education. HE 021 900. 145 pp. MF–$1.07; PC–$14.01.

James, Helen J., and L. Nelson. 1981. "A Classroom Learning Cycle: Using Diagrams to Classify Matter." *Journal of Chemical Education* 58: 476–77.

Johnson, David W., and Roger T. Johnson. 1985. "Classroom Conflict: Controversy versus Debate in Learning Groups." *American Educational Research Journal* 22(2): 237–56.

Johnson, David W., Roger T. Johnson, Edythe J. Holubec, and Patricia Roy. 1984. *Circles of Learning: Cooperation in the Classroom*. Alexandria, Va.: Association for Supervision and Curriculum Development. ED 241 516. 89 pp. MF–$1.07; PC not available EDRS.

Johnson, Ralph H., and J. Anthony Blair. 1980. "The Recent Development of Informal Logic." In *Informal Logic: The First International Symposium*, edited by Ralph H. Johnson and J. Anthony Blair. Inverness, Cal.: Edgepress.

Kahane, Howard. 1980. "The Nature and Classification of Fallacies." In *Informal Logic: The First International Symposium*, edited by R.H. Johnson and J.A. Blair. Inverness, Cal.: Edgepress.

———. 1984. *Logic and Contemporary Rhetoric: The Use of Reason in Everyday Life*. 4th ed. Belmont, Cal.: Wadsworth.

Kahneman, Daniel, Paul Slovic, and Amos Tversky, eds. 1982. *Judgment under Uncertainty: Heuristics and Biases*. New York: Cambridge Univ. Press.

Karplus, Robert. 1974. *Science Curriculum Improvement Study: Teacher's Handbook*. Berkeley: Univ. of California–Berkeley.

———. 1977. "Science Teaching and the Development of Reasoning." *Journal of Research in Science Teaching* 4: 169–75.

Keeley, Stuart M., M. Neil Browne, and Jeffrey S. Kreutzer. 1982. "A Comparison of Freshmen and Seniors on General and Specific Essay Tests of Critical Thinking." *Research in Higher Education* 17(2): 139–54.

Kelly, David. 1988. *The Art of Reasoning*. New York: W.W. Norton.

King, Patricia M.B. 1977. "The Development of Reflective Judgment and Formal Operational Thinking in Adolescents and Young Adults." Ph.D. dissertation, Univ. of Minnesota.

———. 1978. "William Perry's Theory of Intellectual and Ethical Development." In *Applying New Developmental Findings*, edited by Lee Knefelkamp, Carole Widick, and Clyde A. Parker. New Directions for Student Services No. 4. San Francisco: Jossey-Bass.

———. 1985. "Thinking about Critical Thinking: Some New Developments." Paper presented at the National Invitational Conference on Pedagogy and Practice for Student Intellectual Development: High School/College Partnership, Davidson College, June, Davidson, North Carolina.

King, Patricia M., K.S. Kitchener, M.L. Davison, C.A. Parker, and P.K. Wood. 1983. "The Justification of Beliefs in Young Adults: A Longitudinal Study." *Human Development* 26:106–16.

King, Patricia M., K.S. Kitchener, and Phillip K. Wood. 1985. "The Development of Intellect and Character: A Longitudinal-Sequential Study of Intellectual and Moral Development in Young Adults." *Moral Education Forum* 10(1): 1–13.

Kitchener, Karen S. 1977. "Intellectual Development in Late Adolescents and Young Adults: Reflective Judgment and Verbal Reasoning." Ph.D. dissertation, Univ. of Minnesota.

———. 1983. "Cognition, Metacognition, and Epistemic Cognition." *Human Development* 26: 222–32.

Kitchener, Karen S., and Patricia M. King. 1981. "Concepts of Justification and Their Relationship to Age and Education." *Journal of Applied Developmental Psychology* 2: 89–116.

Kneedler, Peter. 1985. "California Assesses Critical Thinking." In *Developing Minds*, edited by Arthur L. Costa. Alexandria, Va.: Association for Supervision and Curriculum Development.

Knefelkamp, L. Lee. 1974. "Developmental Instruction: Fostering Intellectual and Personal Growth of College Students." Doctoral dissertation, Univ. of Minnesota.

Knefelkamp, L. Lee, and William S. Moore. n.d. "Measure of Intellectual Development." Athens, Ga.: Author.

Knefelkamp, L. Lee, and Ron Slepitza. 1976. "A Cognitive Developmental Model of Career Development and Adaptation of the Perry Scheme." *Counseling Psychologist* 6(3): 53–58.

Kogen, Myra. 1986. "The Conventions of Expository Writing." *Journal of Basic Writing* 5(1): 24–37.

Kurfiss, Joanne. 1975. "Late Adolescent Development: A Structural-Epistemological Perspective." Ph.D. dissertation, Univ. of Washington.

————. 1976. "A Neo-Piagetian Analysis of Erikson's 'Identity' Period of Late Adolescent Development." In *Piagetian Research: Compilation and Commentary*, vol. 5, edited by S. Modgil and C. Modgil. Berkshire, Eng.: NFER Publishing.

————. 1977. "Sequentiality and Structure in a Cognitive Model of College Student Development." *Developmental Psychology* 13: 565–71.

————. 1982. "Notes on the Design of Effective Learning Cycles." Proceedings of the Conference on Reasoning, Piaget, and Higher Education. Denver, Colorado.

————. 1987. "Instructional Strategies Inventory." Newark: Univ. of Delaware.

Lanzilotti, S.S. n.d. "Administrating a Thinking Skills Project: A Developmental Perspective." *Teaching Thinking and Problem Solving* 9(3): 16–18.

Larkin, Jill H. 1979. "Information Processing Models and Science Instruction." In *Cognitive Process Instruction: Research on Teaching Thinking Skills*, edited by Jack Lochhead and John Clement. Philadelphia: Franklin Institute Press.

————. 1980. "Teaching Problem Solving in Physics: The Psychological Laboratory and the Practical Classroom." In *Problem Solving and Education: Issues in Teaching and Research*, edited by D.T. Tuma and F. Reif. Hillsdale, N.J.: Erlbaum Associates.

Larkin, Jill H., Joan I. Heller, and James G. Greeno. 1980. "Instructional Implications of Research on Problem Solving." In *Learning, Cognition, and College Teaching*, edited by Wilbert J. McKeachie. New Directions for Teaching and Learning No. 2. San Francisco: Jossey-Bass.

Larkin, Jill H., J. McDermott, D. Simon, and H.A. Simon. 1980. "Expert and Novice Performance in Solving Physics Problems." *Science* 208: 1335–42.

Larkin, J.H., and F. Reif. 1979. "Understanding and Teaching Problem Solving in Physics." *European Journal of Science Education* 1(2): 191–203.

Laveault, Dany, and Pierre Corbeil. 1985. "Educational and Epistemological Foundations of Simulation Games as a Method of Teaching." *Simgames/Simjeux* 11(3 & 4): 20–53.

Lawson, A.E. 1978. "The Development and Validation of a Classroom Test of Formal Reasoning." *Journal of Research in Science Teaching* 15: 11.

Lawson, A.E., and J.W. Renner. 1974. "A Quantitative Analysis of Responses to Piagetian Tasks and Its Implications for Education." *Science Education* 58: 545–59.

Leahy, Rick. 1985. "The Power of the Student Journal." *College Teaching* 33(3): 108–12.

Linn, Marcia C. 1986. "Science." In *Cognition and Instruction*, edited by Ronna F. Dillon and Robert J. Sternberg. New York: Academic Press.

Loacker, Georgine, Lucy Cromwell, Joyce Fey, and Diane Rutherford. 1984. *Analysis and Communication at Alverno: An Approach to Critical Thinking.* Milwaukee: Alverno Productions.

Loacker, Georgine, Lucy Cromwell, and Kathleen O'Brien. 1986. "Assessment in Higher Education: To Serve the Learner." In *Assessment in American Higher Education: Issues and Contexts*, edited by Clifford Adelman. OR 86-301. Washington, D.C.: Office of Educational Research and Improvement. ED 273 197. 90 pp. MF–$1.07; PC–$10.13.

Lochhead, Jack. 1979. "On Learning to Balance Perceptions by Conceptions: A Dialogue between Two Science Students." In *Cognitive Process Instruction*, edited by Jack Lochhead and John Clement. Philadelphia: Franklin Institute Press.

Lochhead, Jack, and Arthur Whimbey. 1987. "Teaching Analytical Reasoning through Thinking-Aloud Pair Problem Solving." In *Developing Critical Thinking and Problem-Solving Abilities*, edited by James E. Stice. New Directions for Teaching and Learning No. 30. San Francisco: Jossey-Bass.

Logan, Ruth. 1987. "Teaching Critical Thinking Using the Scientific Process as a Model System." Santa Monica, Cal. ED 279 384. 12 pp. MF–$1.07; PC–$3.85.

Lord, Charles G., Lee Ross, and Mark R. Leper. 1979. "Biased Assimilation and Attitude Polarization: The Effects of Prior Theories on Subsequently Considered Evidence." *Journal of Personality and Social Psychology* 37(11): 2098–2109.

McKinnon, J.W. 1976. "The College Student and Formal Operations." In *Teaching and Learning with the Piaget Model*, edited by J.W. Renner. Norman: Univ. of Oklahoma Press.

McLeod, Douglas B. 1985. "Affective Issues in Research on Teaching Mathematical Problem Solving." In *Teaching and Learning Mathematical Problem Solving: Multiple Research Perspectives*, edited by Edward A. Silver. Hillsdale, N.J.: Erlbaum Associates.

McMillan, James H. 1987. "Enhancing College Students' Critical Thinking: A Review of Studies." *Research in Higher Education* 26(1): 3–29.

———. 1988. *Assessing Student Learning Outcomes.* New Directions for Teaching and Learning No. 34. San Francisco: Jossey-Bass.

McPeck, John. 1981. *Critical Thinking and Education.* New York: St. Martin's Press.

Malone, Thomas W. 1981. "Toward a Theory of Intrinsically Motivating Instruction." *Cognitive Science* 4: 333–69.

Martinson, Tom L. 1981. "Teaching Effective Thinking with Guided Design in Latin American Geography Courses." *Indiana Social Studies Quarterly* 34(3): 5–14.

Martuza, Victor R. 1987. "Introduction to the Three R's: Reading, Reflecting, and Reacting." Mimeographed. Univ. of Delaware, Dept. of Educational Studies.

Mauksch, Hans O., and C.B. Howery. 1986. "Social Change for Teaching: The Case of One Disciplinary Association." *Teaching Sociology* 14: 73–82.

Mentkowski, Marcia, M. Moeser, and M.J. Strait. 1983. *Using the Perry Scheme of Intellectual and Ethical Development as a College Outcomes Measure: A Process and Criteria for Judging Student Performance.* Milwaukee: Alverno College, Office of Research and Evaluation.

Mentkowski, Marcia, and Glen P. Rogers. 1985. "Longitudinal Assessment of Critical Thinking in College: What Measures Assess Curricular Impact?" Paper presented at the annual meeting of the Mid-Western Educational Research Association, October, Chicago, Illinois.

———. 1986. "Assessing Critical Thinking." In *Teaching Critical Thinking in the Arts and Humanities*, edited by Lucy S. Cromwell. Milwaukee: Alverno Productions.

Meyers, Chet. 1986. *Teaching Students to Think Critically.* San Francisco: Jossey-Bass.

Michaelsen, Larry. 1983. "Team Learning in Large Classes." In *Learning in Groups*, edited by Clark Bouton and Russel Y. Garth. New Directions for Teaching and Learning No. 14. San Francisco: Jossey-Bass.

Michalak, Stanley J., Jr. 1986. "Enhancing Critical-Thinking Skills in Traditional Liberal Arts Courses: Report on a Faculty Workshop." *Liberal Education* 72(3): 253–62.

Miller, Duane I. 1981. *Experience in Decision Making for Students of Industrial Psychology.* Washington, D.C.: Univ. Press of America.

Monk, Stephen G. 1983. "Student Engagement and Teacher Power in Large Classes." In *Learning in Groups*, edited by Clark Bouton and Russel Y. Garth. New Directions for Teaching and Learning No. 14. San Francisco: Jossey-Bass.

Morrill, Richard L. 1980. *Teaching Values in College.* San Francisco: Jossey-Bass.

Mortensen, Lynn, and Willis D. Moreland. 1985. "Critical Thinking in a Freshman Introductory Course: A Case Study." In *To Improve the Academy*, vol. 5, edited by Julie Roy Jeffrey and Glenn R. Erickson. Stillwater, Okla.: POD/New Forums Press.

Muellerleile, Mary Alice. 1986. "Thinking in Images." In *Teaching Critical Thinking in the Arts and Humanities*, edited by Lucy Cromwell. Milwaukee: Alverno Productions.

Muscatine, Charles. September/October 1986. "Faculty Responsibility for the Curriculum." *Academe*: 18–21.

Newell, A., and Herbert A. Simon. 1972. *Human Problem Solving*. Englewood Cliffs, N.J.: Prentice-Hall.

Newell, George. 1984. "Learning from Writing in Two Content Areas: A Case Study/Protocol Analysis." *Research in the Teaching of English* 18(3): 265–87.

Nickerson, Raymond S. 1985. "Understanding Understanding." *American Journal of Education* 93(2): 201–39.

―――. 1986a. "Project Intelligence: An Account and Some Reflections." In *Facilitating Cognitive Development: International Perspectives, Programs, and Practices*, edited by M. Schwebel and C.A. Maher. New York: Haworth.

―――. 1986b. "Reasoning." In *Cognition and Instruction*, edited by Ronna F. Dillon and Robert J. Sternberg. New York: Academic Press.

―――. 1986c. "Why Teach Thinking?" In *Teaching Thinking Skills: Theory and Practice*, edited by Joan B. Baron and Robert J. Sternberg. New York: W.H. Freeman.

Nickerson, Raymond S., David N. Perkins, and Edward E. Smith. 1985. *The Teaching of Thinking*. Hillsdale, N.J.: Erlbaum Associates.

Nisbett, Richard E., Geoffrey T. Fong, Darrin R. Lehman, and Patricia W. Cheng. October 1987. "Teaching Reasoning." *Science* 238: 625–31.

Norton, Sylvia, and others. 1985. "The Effects of an Independent Laboratory Investigation on the Critical Thinking Ability and Scientific Attitudes of Students in a General Microbiology Class." Paper presented at the annual meeting of the Mid-South Research Association, November, Biloxi, Mississippi. ED 264 291. 18 pp. MF–$1.07; PC–$3.85.

Organ, T.W. 1965. *The Art of Critical Thinking*. Boston: Houghton Mifflin.

Palincsar, Annamarie S., and Ann L. Brown. 1984. "Reciprocal Teaching of Comprehension Fostering and Comprehension Monitoring Activities." *Cognition and Instruction* 1(2): 117–75.

Palmer, Parker J. 1987. "Community, Conflict, and Ways of Knowing: Ways to Deepen Our Educational Agenda." *Change* 19(5): 20–25.

Pascarella, Eugene T. 1980. "Student-Faculty Informal Contact and College Outcomes." *Review of Educational Research* 50: 545–95.

Paul, Richard. 1982. "Teaching Critical Thinking in the 'Strong' Sense: A Focus on Self-Deception, World Views, and a Dialectical Mode of Analysis." *Informal Logic* 4: 3–7.

―――. 1986. "Dialogical Thinking: Critical Thought Essential to the Acquisition of Rational Knowledge and Passions." In *Teaching Thinking Skills*, edited by Joan B. Baron and Robert J. Sternberg. New York: W.H. Freeman.

Perfetto, Greg A., John D. Bransford, and Jeffery J. Franks. 1983. "Constraints on Access in a Problem-Solving Context." *Memory and Cognition* 11(1): 24–31.

Perkins, David N. 1981. *The Mind's Best Work*. Cambridge, Mass.: Harvard Univ. Press.

———. 1985. "Postprimary Education Has Little Impact on Informal Reasoning." *Journal of Educational Psychology* 77(5): 562–71.

———. 1986. "Reasoning as It Is and Could Be: An Empirical Perspective." Paper presented at the annual conference of the American Educational Research Association, April, San Francisco, California.

Perkins, D.N., R. Allen, and J. Hafner. 1983. "Difficulties in Everyday Reasoning." In *Thinking: The Expanding Frontier*, edited by William Maxwell. Proceedings of the International, Interdisciplinary Conference on Thinking held at the Univ. of the South Pacific, January 1982. Philadelphia: Franklin Institute Press.

Perry, William G., Jr. 1970. *Forms of Intellectual and Ethical Development in the College Years: A Scheme*. New York: Holt, Rinehart.

———. 1981. "Cognitive and Ethical Growth: The Making of Meaning." In *The Modern American College,* edited by Arthur Chickering. San Francisco: Jossey-Bass.

Piaget, Jean. 1968. "The Role of the Concept of Equilibration in Psychological Explication." In *Six Psychological Studies*, edited by David Elkind. New York: Vintage Books.

Pittendrigh, Adele S., and Patrick C. Jobes 1984. "Teaching across the Curriculum: Critical Communication in the Sociology Classroom." *Teaching Sociology* 11(3): 281–96.

Polya, G. 1957. *How to Solve It: A New Aspect of Mathematical Method*. Garden City, N.Y.: Doubleday/Anchor Books.

Postman, Neil. 1985a. *Amusing Ourselves to Death: Public Discourse in the Age of Entertainment*. New York: Viking.

———. 1985b. "Critical Thinking in the Electronic Era." *National Forum* 65(1): 4–8 +.

Powers, Donald E., and Mary K. Enright. 1987. "Analytical Reasoning Skills in Graduate Study: Perceptions of Faculty in Six Fields." *Journal of Higher Education* 58(6): 658–82.

Reinsmith, William A. 1987. "Educating for Change: A Teacher Has Second Thoughts." *College Teaching* 35(3): 83–88.

Resnick, Lauren B. 1987. *Education and Learning to Think*. Washington, D.C.: National Academy Press.

Riordan, Timothy. 1986. "Obstacles to the Development of Critical Thinking and Ways to Overcome Them." In *Teaching Critical*

Thinking in Arts and Humanities, edited by Lucy Cromwell. Milwaukee: Alverno Productions.

Roby, Thomas W. 1983. "The Other Side of Questioning: Controversial Turns, the Devil's Advocate, and the Reflective Student Responses." Paper presented at the annual meeting of the American Educational Research Association, April, Montreal, Ontario.

———. 1985. "The Problematics of Classroom Discussion." Paper presented at the annual meeting of the American Educational Research Association, April, Chicago, Illinois.

Ross, Lee, and Craig A. Anderson. 1982. "Shortcomings in the Attribution Process: On the Origins and Maintenance of Erroneous Social Assessments." In *Judgment under Uncertainty: Heuristics and Biases*, edited by Daniel Kahneman, Paul Slovic, and Amos Tversky. New York: Cambridge Univ. Press.

Rubinstein, Moshe F. 1975. *Patterns of Problem Solving*. Englewood Cliffs, N.J.: Prentice-Hall.

———. 1980. "A Decade of Experience in Teaching an Interdisciplinary Problem-Solving Course." In *Problem Solving and Education: Issues in Teaching and Research*, edited by D.T. Tuma and F. Reif. Hillsdale, N.J.: Erlbaum Associates.

———. 1986. *Tools for Thinking and Problem Solving*. Englewood Cliffs, N.J.: Prentice-Hall.

Rubinstein, Moshe F., and Iris R. Firstenberg. 1987. "Tools for Thinking." In *Developing Critical Thinking and Problem-Solving Abilities*, edited by James E. Stice. New Directions for Teaching and Learning No. 30. San Francisco: Jossey-Bass.

Ruggierio, Vincent R. 1984. *The Art of Thinking: A Guide to Critical and Creative Thought*. New York: Harper & Row.

Rumelhart, D.E. 1977. *Introduction to Human Information Processing*. New York: John Wiley & Sons.

Ryan, Mary Ann, Donald Robinson, and J.W. Carmichael, Jr. 1980. "A Piagetian-Based General Chemistry Laboratory Program for Science Majors." *Journal of Chemical Education* 57(9): 642–45.

Ryan, Michael P. 1984a. "Conceptions of Prose Coherence: Individual Differences in Epistemological Standards." *Journal of Educational Psychology* 76(6): 1226–38.

———. 1984b. "Monitoring Text Comprehension: Individual Differences in Epistemological Standards." *Journal of Educational Psychology* 76(2): 248–58.

Sanford, Nevitt. 1966. *Self and Society: Social Change and Individual Development*. New York: Atherton Press.

Scardamalia, Marlene, and Carl Bereiter. 1986. "Writing." In *Cognition and Instruction*, edited by Ronna F. Dillon and Robert J. Sternberg. New York: Academic Press.

Schank, R.C., and R. Abelson. 1977. *Scripts, Plans, Goals, and Understanding*. Hillsdale, N.J.: Erlbaum Associates.

Schlaefli, Andre, James R. Rest, and Stephen J. Thoma. 1985. "Does Moral Education Improve Moral Judgment? A Meta-Analysis of Intervention Studies Using the Defining Issues Test." *Review of Educational Research* 55(3): 319–52.

Schmidt, Jane A., and Mark L. Davison. 1983. "Helping Students Think." *Personnel and Guidance Journal* 61(9): 563–69.

Schmidt, Julie A., John P. McLaughlin, and Patricia Leighten. n.d. "Novice Strategies for Understanding Paintings." *Applied Cognitive Psychology*. In press.

Schoenfeld, Allen H. 1983a. "Beyond the Purely Cognitive: Belief Systems, Social Cognitions, and Metacognitions as Driving Forces in Intellectual Performance." *Cognitive Science* 7: 329–63.

———. 1983b. *Problem Solving in the Mathematics Curriculum: A Report, Recommendations, and an Annotated Bibliography.* M.A.A. Notes No. 1. Washington, D.C.: Mathematical Association of America.

———. 1985a. *Mathematical Problem Solving.* New York: Academic Press.

———. 1985b. "Metacognitive and Epistemological Issues in Mathematical Understanding." In *Teaching and Learning Mathematical Problem Solving: Multiple Research Perspectives*, edited by Edward A. Silver. Hillsdale, N.J.: Erlbaum Associates.

Schoenfeld, Allen H., and Douglas J. Herrmann. 1982. "Problem Perception and Knowledge Structure in Expert and Novice Mathematical Problem Solvers." *Journal of Experimental Psychology: Learning, Memory, and Cognition* 8(5): 484–94.

Schon, Donald. 1983. *The Reflective Practitioner.* New York: Basic Books.

———. 1987. *Educating the Reflective Practitioner.* San Francisco: Jossey-Bass.

Scriven, Michael. 1980. "Prescriptive and Descriptive Approaches to Problem Solving." In *Problem Solving and Education: Issues in Teaching and Research*, edited by D.T. Tuma and F. Reif. Hillsdale, N.J.: Erlbaum Associates.

Shor, Ira. 1980. *Critical Teaching and Everyday Life.* Boston: South End Press.

———, ed. 1987. *Freire for the Classroom: A Sourcebook for Liberatory Teaching.* Portsmouth, N.H.: Heinemann Educational Books.

Shulman, L.S., and N.B. Carey. 1984. "Psychology and the Limitations of Individual Rationality: Implications for the Study of Reasoning and Civility." *Review of Educational Research* 54(4): 501–24.

Simon, Dorothea P., and Herbert A. Simon. 1979. "A Tale of Two Protocols." In *Cognitive Process Instruction*, edited by J. Lochhead and John Clement. Philadelphia: Franklin Institute Press.

Simon, Herbert A. 1980. "Problem Solving and Education." In *Prob-

lem Solving and Education: Issues in Teaching and Research, edited by D.T. Tuma and F. Reif. Hillsdale, N.J.: Erlbaum Associates.

Slater, Wayne H., Michael Graves, Sherry B. Scott, and Teresa M. Redd-Boyd. 1988. "Discourse Structure and College Freshmen's Recall Production of Expository Text." *Research in the Teaching of English* 22(1): 45–61.

Smith, Daryl G. 1977. "College Classroom Interactions and Critical Thinking." *Journal of Educational Psychology* 69: 180–90.

Sommers, Nancy. 1980. "Revision Strategies of Student Writers and Experienced Adult Writers." *College Composition and Communication* 31(4): 378–91.

Spilich, G.J., G.T. Vesonder, H.L. Chiesi, and J.F. Voss. 1979. "Text Processing of Domain-Related Information for Individuals with High and Low Domain Knowledge." *Journal of Verbal Learning and Verbal Behavior* 18: 275–90.

Spurlin, Joni E., Donald F. Dansereau, Celia O. Larson, and Larry W. Brooks. 1984 "Cooperative Learning Strategies in Processing Descriptive Text: Effects of Role and Activity Level of the Learner." *Cognition and Instruction* 1(4): 451–63.

Stark, Jerry. 1987. "On Academic Preconditions of Critical Theory: Conditions, Possibilities, and Proposals." Paper prepared for the annual meeting of the Midwest Sociological Society, April, Chicago, Illinois.

Stasz, Bird B., and Associates. 1985. "A Problem-Solving Model for Teaching Reading Proficiency." *Forum for Reading* 16(2): 56–60. ED 262 377. 7 pp. MF–$1.07; PC–$3.85.

Statkiewicz, Walter R., and Robert D. Allen. 1983. "Practice Exercises to Develop Critical Thinking Skills." *Journal of College Science Teaching* 12(4): 262–66.

Stephenson, Bud W., and Christine Hunt. 1977. "Intellectual and Ethical Development: A Dualistic Curriculum Intervention for College Students." *Counseling Psychologist* 6(4): 39–42.

Stern, G.C., and A.H. Cope. 1956. "Differences in Educability between Stereopaths, Nonstereopaths, and Rationals." Cited in Philip E. Jacob, *Changing Values in College: An Exploratory Study of the Impact of College Teaching*. New York: Harper & Row.

Stevens, Albert L., and Dedre Gentner. 1983. "Introduction." In *Mental Models*, edited by Dedre Gentner and Albert L. Stevens. Hillsdale, N.J.: Erlbaum Associates.

Stonewater, Jerry, and Harry M. Daniels. 1983. "Psychosocial and Cognitive Development in a Career Decision-making Course." *Journal of College Student Personnel* 24: 403–10.

Swaffer, Janet K. 1986. "Reading and Cultural Literacy." *Journal of General Education* 38(2): 70–84.

Swartz, Robert J. 1986. "Teaching for Thinking: A Developmental

Model for the Infusion of Thinking Skills into Mainstream Instruction." In *Teaching Thinking Skills: Theory and Practice*, edited by Joan B. Baron and Robert J. Sternberg. New York: W.H. Freeman.

Terrio, Susan J. 1986. "Building Critical Thinking Skills through Writing in the Foreign Language Classroom." Paper presented at the annual meeting of the Northeast Conference on the Teaching of Foreign Languages, April, Washington, D.C. ED 276 263. 16 pp. MF–$1.07; PC–$3.85.

Tomlinson-Keasey, Carol, and Debra C. Eisert. 1978. "Can Doing Promote Thinking in the College Classroom?" *Journal of College Student Personnel* 19: 99–105.

Touchton, Judith G., Loretta C. Wertheimer, Janet L. Cornfeld, and Karen H. Harrison. 1977. "Career Planning and Decision Making: A Developmental Approach to the Classroom." *Counseling Psychologist* 6(4): 42–47.

Toulmin, Stephen E. 1958. *The Uses of Argument*. Cambridge, Eng.: Cambridge Univ. Press.

Toulmin, Stephen, Richard Rieke, and Allan Janik. 1979. *An Introduction to Reasoning*. New York: Macmillan.

Tweeney, R.D. 1981. "Confirmatory and Disconfirmatory Heuristics in Michael Faraday's Scientific Research." Paper presented at a meeting of the Psychonomic Society. Cited in Voss, Greene, Post, and Penner 1983.

VanDeWeghe, Rick. 1986. "From Problem Solving to Problem Finding through Purposeful, Informal Writing." Paper presented at the Annual Conference on College Composition and Communication, New Orleans, Louisiana.

Verderber, Rudolph. 1967. "Teaching Reasoning in the Beginning High School and College Speech Course." *Ohio Speech Journal* 5: 26–32.

Vosniadou, Stella, and William F. Brewer. 1987. "Theories of Knowledge Restructuring in Development." *Review of Educational Research* 57(1): 51–68.

Voss, J.F., J. Blais, M.L. Means, T.R. Greene, and E. Ahwesh. 1986. "Informal Reasoning and Subject Matter Knowledge in the Solving of Economics Problems by Naive and Novice Individuals." *Cognition and Instruction* 3(4): 269–302.

Voss, James F., Terry R. Greene, Timothy A. Post, and Barbara C. Penner. 1983. "Problem-Solving Skill in the Social Sciences." *The Psychology of Learning and Motivation: Advances in Research and Theory*, vol. 17, edited by G.H. Bower. New York: Academic Press.

Voss, James F., Sherman W. Tyler, and Laurie A. Yengo. 1983. "Individual Differences in the Solving of Social Science Problems." In *Individual Differences in Cognition*, vol. 1, edited by R.F. Dillon and R.R. Schmeck. New York: Academic Press.

Vygotsky, Lev. 1978. *Mind in Society: The Development of Higher Psychological Processes*, edited by Michael Cole, Vera John-Steiner, Sylvia Scribner, and Ellen Souberman. Cambridge, Mass.: Harvard Univ. Press.

Wales, Charles E. 1979. "Does How You Teach Make a Difference?" *Engineering Education* 69(5): 394–98.

Wales, Charles E., Anne H. Nardi, and Robert A. Stager. 1986. *Professional Decision Making*. Morgantown, W. Va.: Univ. Center for Guided Design.

Walters, Kerry S. 1986. "Critical Thinking in Liberal Education: A Case of Overkill?" *Liberal Education* 72(3): 233–44.

Watson, G., and E.M. Glaser. 1980. "The Watson-Glaser Critical Thinking Appraisal." Cleveland: Psychology Corporation.

Weinstein, Claire, and Brenda Rogers. 1985. "Comprehension Monitoring: The Neglected Learning Strategy." *Journal of Developmental Education* 9(1): 6 –9 +.

Welfel, Elizabeth R. November 1982. "How Students Make Judgments: Do Educational Level and Academic Major Make a Difference?" *Journal of College Student Personnel* 23(6): 490 –97.

Whimbey, Arthur, J.W. Carmichael, Jr., Lester W. Jones, Jacqueline T. Hunter, and Harold A. Vincent. October 1980. "Teaching Critical Reading and Analytical Reasoning in Project SOAR." *Journal of Reading* 24(1): 5–10.

Whimbey, Arthur, and Jack Lochhead. 1979. *Problem Solving and Comprehension: A Short Course in Analytical Reasoning*. Philadelphia: Franklin Institute Press.

———. 1982. *Problem Solving and Comprehension*. 3d ed. Philadelphia: Franklin Institute Press.

White, Edward M. 1984. "Holisticism." *College Composition and Communication* 35(4): 400 – 409.

———. 1985. *Teaching and Assessing Writing*. San Francisco: Jossey-Bass.

Whitman, Neal A., David C. Spendlove, and Claire H. Clark. 1984. *Student Stress: Effects and Solutions*. ASHE-ERIC Higher Education Report No. 2. Washington, D.C.: Association for the Study of Higher Education. ED 246 832. 115 pp. MF–$1.07; PC–$12.07.

———. 1986. *Increasing Students' Learning: A Faculty Guide to Reducing Stress among Students*. ASHE-ERIC Higher Education Report No. 4. Washington, D.C.: Association for the Study of Higher Education. ED 274 264. 101 pp. MF–$1.07; PC–$12.07.

Widick, Carole. 1975. *An Evaluation of Developmental Instruction*. Doctoral dissertation, Univ. of Minnesota.

Widick, Carole L., L. Lee Knefelkamp, and Clyde A. Parker. 1975. "The Counselor as a Developmental Instructor." *Counselor Education and Supervision* 14: 286 –96.

Widick, Carole, and Debra Simpson. 1978. "Developmental Concepts in College Instruction." In *Encouraging Development in College Students*, edited by Clyde A. Parker. Minneapolis: Univ. of Minnesota Press.

Winter, David G., David C. McClelland, and Abigail J. Stewart. 1981. *A New Case for the Liberal Arts*. San Francisco: Jossey-Bass.

Wolters, Richard. 1986. "Critical Thinking and Transference across Time." In *Teaching Critical Thinking in Arts and Humanities*, edited by Lucy Cromwell. Milwaukee: Alverno Productions.

Wulff, Donald, and Jody Nyquist. 1988. "Using Field Methods as an Instructional Tool." In *To Improve the Academy*, vol. 7, edited by Joanne Kurfiss, Linda Hilsen, Susan Kahn, Mary Deane Sorcinelli, and Richard Tiberius. Stillwater, Okla.: POD/New Forums Press.

Zeichner, Kenneth M., and Daniel P. Liston. 1987. "Teaching Student Teachers to Reflect." *Harvard Educational Review* 57(1): 23–48.

Zeuli, John S., and Margret Buchmann. 1986. "Implementation of Teacher Thinking Research as Curriculum Deliberation." Occasional Paper No. 107. East Lansing: Michigan State Univ., Institute for Research on Teaching. ED 275 644. 27 pp. MF–$1.07; PC–$5.79.

INDEX

A

General College Program, 96, 100
General education courses, 94
General Liberal Education Program (GLEP), 92, 96
Generalization, 16
Glaser, Edward M., 7-8, 10
GLEP (see General Liberal Education Program)
Good Reason for Writing, 18
Grade point average, 44, 75
Grading
    "holistic scoring," 88
    model, 77
    understanding criteria, 87
Grime, Larry, 97
Guided Learning/design, 73, 75

H

Harvard developmental studies, 51, 57
Hays, Janice N., 59
Hierarchies
    instructional use, 48
    structure of knowledge, 36-37
Historical background, 7-11
History
    analysis of, 37
    declarative knowledge acquisition, 36
    instruction, 81-82
Humanities instructions, 76-81

I

Identification, 57
Individual development, 56-57
Induction: informal arguments, 14-15
Informal Logic, 17
Informality: logic/reasoning, 14-16
Inhelder, Barbel, 9
Inquiry methods, 35-36, 41, 47, 48
Institutional programs: early, 9-10
Instruction
    critical thinking courses, 88-89
    declarative knowledge implications, 38-39
    goals, 101
    humanities, 76-81
    inquiry approach, 35-36
    metacognition implications, 42-46
    sciences/mathematics/engineering, 71-76
    social sciences, 81-85

problem-solving strategies, 71-72
vs. expert reasoning processes, 30-33

O
Objectivity development, 45
Opinions, 54
Organization
    declarative knowledge, 36-37
    instruction, 39
    memory, 26-27, 34
Organizational change, 97
Organizational strategies
    formal/institutionally sponsored, 98-100
    informal, 97-98
    types, 97

P
Peers
    faculty collaboration, 1045
    teaching, 47, 73, 76, 79
Perry, William, 51, 52
Perry development model, 11, 55, 58-60, 86, 97
Persistence, 44, 75, 93
Philosophy
    instruction, 78-79
    perspectives, 5
Physics
    declarative knowledge acquisition, 36
    problem solving, 32
    procedural knowledge, 40
Piagetian approach, 9-10, 34, 44, 93
Planning: metacognition, 43
Political science
    instruction, 82
    problem solving, 32-33
    procedural knowledge, 40
Practice, 48
Prefreshman skill development, 71-72
Pretests, 39
Problem solving
    art history, 32
    composition, 31-32
    critical thinking as, 28-30
    declarative knowledge, 33-39
    mathematics, 31
    metacognition, 42-46

field work, 84
identification, 57
integration with reasoning, 18, 81
journal entries, 77
mastering information, 38-39
quality, 62
sequenced instruction, 62
usefulness of, 86
Writing Across the Curriculum, 98

X

Xavier University
SOAR program, 11, 44, 71-72, 93

Z

Zorba the Greek, 80

ASHE-ERIC HIGHER EDUCATION REPORTS

Since 1983, the Association for the Study of Higher Education (ASHE) and the ERIC Clearinghouse on Higher Education, a sponsored project of the School of Education and Human Development at the George Washington University, have cosponsored the ASHE-ERIC Higher Education Report series. The 1988 series is the seventeenth overall, with the American Association for Higher Education having served as cosponsor before 1983.

Each monograph is the definitive analysis of a tough higher education problem, based on thorough research of pertinent literature and institutional experiences. After topics are identified by a national survey, noted practitioners and scholars write the reports, with experts reviewing each manuscript before publication.

Eight monographs (10 monographs before 1985) in the ASHE-ERIC Higher Education Report series are published each year, available individually or by subscription. Subscription to eight issues is $60 regular; $50 for members of AERA, AAHE, and AIR; $40 for members of ASHE (add $10.00 for postage outside the United States).

Prices for single copies, including 4th class postage and handling, are $15.00 regular and $11.25 for members of AERA, AAHE, AIR, and ASHE ($10.00 regular and $7.50 for members for 1985 to 1987 reports, $7.50 regular and $6.00 for members for 1983 and 1984 reports, $6.50 regular and $5.00 for members for reports published before 1983). If faster postage is desired for U.S. and Canadian orders, add $1.00 for each publication ordered; overseas, add $5.00. For VISA and MasterCard payments, include card number, expiration date, and signature. Orders under $25 must be prepaid. Bulk discounts are available on orders of 15 or more reports (not applicable to subscriptions). Order from the Publications Department, ASHE-ERIC Higher Education Reports, The George Washington University, One Dupont Circle, Suite 630, Washington, D.C. 20036-1183, or phone us at 202/296-2597. Write for a publications list of all the Higher Education Reports available.

1988 ASHE-ERIC Higher Education Reports

1. The Invisible Tapestry: Culture in American Colleges and Universities
   George D. Kuh and Elizabeth J. Whitt

2. Critical Thinking: Theory, Research, Practice, and Possibilities
   Joanne Gainen Kurfiss

1987 ASHE-ERIC Higher Education Reports

1. Incentive Early Retirement Programs for Faculty: Innovative Responses to a Changing Environment
   Jay L. Chronister and Thomas R. Kepple, Jr.

2. Working Effectively with Trustees: Building Cooperative Campus Leadership
   Barbara E. Taylor

3. Formal Recognition of Employer-Sponsored Instruction: Conflict and Collegiality in Postsecondary Education
   Nancy S. Nash and Elizabeth M. Hawthorne

4. Learning Styles: Implications for Improving Educational Practices
   Charles S. Claxton and Patricia H. Murrell

5. Higher Education Leadership: Enhancing Skills through Professional

Development Programs
Sharon A. McDade

6. Higher Education and the Public Trust: Improving Stature in Colleges and Universities
Richard L. Alfred and Julie Weissman

7. College Student Outcomes Assessment: A Talent Development Perspective
Maryann Jacobi, Alexander Astin, and Frank Ayala, Jr.

8. Opportunity from Strength: Strategic Planning Clarified with Case Examples
Robert G. Cope

1986 ASHE-ERIC Higher Education Reports

1. Post-tenure Faculty Evaluation: Threat or Opportunity?
Christine M. Licata

2. Blue Ribbon Commissions and Higher Education: Changing Academe from the Outside
Janet R. Johnson and Lawrence R. Marcus

3. Responsive Professional Education: Balancing Outcomes and Opportunities
Joan S. Stark, Malcolm A. Lowther, and Bonnie M.K. Hagerty

4. Increasing Students' Learning: A Faculty Guide to Reducing Stress among Students
Neal A. Whitman, David C. Spendlove, and Claire H. Clark

5. Student Financial Aid and Women: Equity Dilemma?
Mary Moran

6. The Master's Degree: Tradition, Diversity, Innovation
Judith S. Glazer

7. The College, the Constitution, and the Consumer Student: Implications for Policy and Practice
Robert M. Hendrickson and Annette Gibbs

8. Selecting College and University Personnel: The Quest and the Questions
Richard A. Kaplowitz

1985 ASHE-ERIC Higher Education Reports

1. Flexibility in Academic Staffing: Effective Policies and Practices
Kenneth P. Mortimer, Marque Bagshaw, and Andrew T. Masland

2. Associations in Action: The Washington, D.C., Higher Education Community
Harland G. Bloland

3. And on the Seventh Day: Faculty Consulting and Supplemental Income
Carol M. Boyer and Darrell R. Lewis

4. Faculty Research Performance: Lessons from the Sciences and Social Sciences
John W. Creswell

5. Academic Program Reviews: Institutional Approaches, Expectations, and

Controversies
Clifton F. Conrad and Richard F. Wilson

6. Students in Urban Settings: Achieving the Baccalaureate Degree
Richard C. Richardson, Jr., and Louis W. Bender

7. Serving More Than Students: A Critical Need for College Student Personnel Services
Peter H. Garland

8. Faculty Participation in Decision Making: Necessity or Luxury?
Carol E. Floyd

1984 ASHE-ERIC Higher Education Reports

1. Adult Learning: State Policies and Institutional Practices
K. Patricia Cross and Anne-Marie McCartan

2. Student Stress: Effects and Solutions
Neal A. Whitman, David C. Spendlove, and Claire H. Clark

3. Part-time Faculty: Higher Education at a Crossroads
Judith M. Gappa

4. Sex Discrimination Law in Higher Education: The Lessons of the Past Decade
J. Ralph Lindgren, Patti T. Ota, Perry A. Zirkel, and Nan Van Gieson

5. Faculty Freedoms and Institutional Accountability: Interactions and Conflicts
Steven G. Olswang and Barbara A. Lee

6. The High-Technology Connection: Academic/Industrial Cooperation for Economic Growth
Lynn G. Johnson

7. Employee Educational Programs: Implications for Industry and Higher Education
Suzanne W. Morse

8. Academic Libraries: The Changing Knowledge Centers of Colleges and Universities
Barbara B. Moran

9. Futures Research and the Strategic Planning Process: Implications for Higher Education
James L. Morrison, William L. Renfro, and Wayne I. Boucher

10. Faculty Workload: Research, Theory, and Interpretation
Harold E. Yuker

1983 ASHE-ERIC Higher Education Reports

1. The Path to Excellence: Quality Assurance in Higher Education
Laurence R. Marcus, Anita O. Leone, and Edward D. Goldberg

2. Faculty Recruitment, Retention, and Fair Employment: Obligations and Opportunities
John S. Waggaman

3. Meeting the Challenges: Developing Faculty Careers*
Michael C.T. Brookes and Katherine L. German

*Out-of-print. Available through EDRS.

*Out-of-print. Available through EDRS.

Order Form

QUANTITY   AMOUNT

_____ Please enter my subscription to the 1988 ASHE-ERIC
      Higher Education Reports at $60.00, 50% off the cover
      price, beginning with Report 1, 1988.   _____

_____ Please enter my subscription to the 1989 ASHE-ERIC
      Higher Education Reports at $80.00, 33% off the cover
      price, beginning with Report 1, 1989.   _____

_____ Outside U.S., add $10.00 per series for postage.   _____

Individual reports are available at the following prices:
1988 and forward, $15.00 per copy.   1983 and 1984, $7.50 per copy.
1985 to 1987, $10.00 per copy.   1982 and back, $6.50 per copy.

Book rate postage, U.S. only, is included in the price.
For fast U.P.S. shipping within the U.S., add $1.00 per book.
Outside U.S., please add $1.00 per book for surface shipping.
For air mail service outside U.S., add $5.00 per book.
All orders under $25 must be prepaid.

PLEASE SEND ME THE FOLLOWING REPORTS:

QUANTITY   TITLE   AMOUNT
_____ Report NO. ____ (_____)   _____
_____ Report NO. ____ (_____)   _____
_____ Report NO. ____ (_____)   _____
                                   SUBTOTAL: _____
               POSTAGE (see above) _____
          TOTAL AMOUNT DUE: _____

Please check one of the following:

☐ Check enclosed, payable to ASHE.
☐ Purchase order attached.
☐ Charge my credit card indicated below:
               ☐ VISA   ☐ MasterCard

```
┌─┬─┬─┬─┬─┬─┬─┬─┬─┬─┬─┬─┬─┬─┬─┬─┐
│ │ │ │ │ │ │ │ │ │ │ │ │ │ │ │ │
└─┴─┴─┴─┴─┴─┴─┴─┴─┴─┴─┴─┴─┴─┴─┴─┘
```

Expiration date _____

Name _____

Title _____

Institution _____

Address _____

City _____ State _____ Zip _____

Phone _____ Signature _____

ALL ORDERS SHOULD BE SENT TO:
ASHE-ERIC Higher Education Reports
The George Washington University
One Dupont Circle, Suite 630, Dept. RC
Washington, DC 20036-1183
Phone: 202/296-2597